A CULTURE OF MINISTERING

Leading the Relief Society & Elders Quorum to Minister Unto *His* People

KURT FRANCOM

LEADING**SAINTS**
BE A LEADER - NOT A CALLING

KURT FRANCOM

A Culture of Ministering

Leading the Relief Society and
Elders Quorum to Minister Unto
His People

KURT FRANCOM

Copyright © 2018 by Kurt Francom.
All rights reserved. No part of this book may be reproduced in any form or by any electronic or mechanical means including information storage and retrieval systems – except in the case of brief quotations in articles or reviews—without the permission in writing from its publisher, Kurt Francom.
All brand names and product names used in this book are trademarks, registered trademarks, or trade names of their respective holders. Leading Saints is not associated with any product or vendor in this book.
This work is not an official publication of The Church of Jesus Christ of Latter-day Saints. The views expressed herein are the responsibility of the author and do not necessarily represent the position of the Church.

10 9 8 7 6 5 4 3 2 1

Kurt Francom
Leading Saints
Salt Lake City, Utah
LeadingSaints.org

ISBN: 9781791817114

DEDICATION

To Mom—who has been quietly ministering her entire life.

CONTENTS

Introduction		1
Chapter 1	**Start With Vision**	7
	Prepare Their Minds by Articulating the Issue	11
		15
	Creating a Vision Statement	21
	Vision Statements Take Time	22
	Building a Culture Around the Vision	23
Chapter 2	**Get Organized**	29
	The Calling Monster	31
	Delegate, Delegate, Delegate	33
	Make it Easy	36
	Appointment Management	46
	Only the President	47
Chapter 3	**Ministering Interviews**	49
	Consistency is Key	52
	But What About…?	57
	Conducting Ministering Interviews	61
	Learn Their Name	62
	Prepare Their Minds	63
	The Interview	66
	All This in 15 Minutes?	72
	Onboarding	73
	Ministering Interviews are First downs, not Touchdowns	74
	Bring an Extra Chair	76
Chapter 4	**Led by the Spirit**	79
	Establishing Structure	81

	Feeding the Fire	83
	101 Ways to Minister	84
	Many Don't Need Ministering Brothers or Sisters	88
	Introverts	90
	"They're Fine"	97
	Conclusion	98
Chapter 5	**Motivating Saints**	**101**
	Fundamental Attribution Error	102
	Is There REALLY a Motivation Problem?	105
	Influencing Change	111
	Source 1 – Personal Motivation	113
	Source 2 – Personal Ability	116
	Sources 3 & 4 – Harness Peer Pressure & Finding Strength in Numbers	118
	Source 5 – Design Rewards and Demand Accountablility	120
	Source 6 – Change the Environment	121
	Establishing a Ministering Strategy	123
	A Word on Unity	126
Conclusion		**129**
Epilogue		**133**
	About the Author	**135**

ACKNOWLEDGMENTS

I sincerely thank my youth leaders who first taught me the power of ministering through the home teaching program; Wayne Mackay, Ken Christopher, Wayne Magleby, Ken Searle, Kent Evans, of course, my father, Rick Francom, and many more in the original Taylorsville 24th ward. The Leading Saints community, especially those in the Leading Saints Helpers Facebook group.

David DeFord for his constant encouragement and for reviewing my original draft that was based on the home/visiting teaching program.

Steve Asvitt for being a remarkable editor and spending countless hours reviewing and helping my message be more clear and helpful. Ken Williams for helping me get this book into a physical copy.

Tevya Washburn and Rebecca Buxton, members of the Leading Saints board who have been so supportive in all the projects we have taken on in order to help leaders across the world.

Of course, my wife, Alanna, who allowed me to seclude myself in a dark room so that I could articulate the sentences that follow.

INTRODUCTION

As a young teacher in the Aaronic priesthood, I remember receiving a call from the ward executive secretary asking me to meet with Bishop Mackay after church the following Sunday. I was used to regular youth interviews so I figured it would be another checkup making sure I wasn't getting too off track as a teenager.

Sitting in his bishop's office, I was surprised to hear him say, "Brother Francom, we have a new calling for you." At this point, I just let out a classic teenager grunt to let him know I was listening. "We'd like to call you as the priesthood chorister."

"Okay, sure."

Bishop Mackay continued, "This would require you to select a hymn at the beginning of each priesthood opening exercises and then stand in front of all the brethren attending and lead the music."

I had seen people wave their arm to the music before so I figured it wasn't advanced calculus. I barely played the piano. In fact, I think I had recently quit piano lessons. So I had a little music knowledge to reference.

For the next several years, as I developed as a young priesthood holder, I also developed as a chorister.

However, there was something interesting about the role as chorister that I learned rather quickly after being called: Nobody really watched my flailing arm. I could slow down the beat with my arm, but the pianist would continue playing the song at whatever tempo he wanted. I could stop waving my arm and walk out of the room, but it would not leave anyone confused or seeking a new chorister. They called me the chorister but nobody was following. Fourteen years later I was called as the bishop of a ward down the street in South Salt Lake. I would often look over a sacrament meeting agenda or a baptismal program and fret that we needed someone to lead the music. It seems part of our Latter-day Saint culture to mandate someone stand in front of the singing group and wave their arm as if the roof will fall in if we don't have a chorister in front of the room while singing.

I remember one particular Sunday when I was presiding over a sacrament meeting. In my haste to make sure speakers were present and that we were starting on time, I failed to realize our sacrament meeting chorister hadn't arrived. We came to the first hymn, and guess what? Everyone sang without missing a beat, and it sounded great! I think others were uncomfortable with straying from tradition because the ward Relief Society president finally abandoned her family in the pews and led the remaining verses of that hymn and all hymns that followed in the meeting.

Leading music in the church can be a metaphor for how we lead in other church callings. We always make sure someone is called and set apart as a leader of the Relief Society or an elders quorum, but that doesn't mean people are following along. The leader slips into the role and stands each week to "welcome" those attending and then rattles off a few announcements. But does the group really look to the leader for direction? Inspiration? Vision? Most in attendance are attending for reasons other than to follow, and they typically set their own tempo and carry on as they wish.

What results is a Relief Society or elders quorum tempo that is out of sync for everyone. This results in leadership music that has no power to change the heart of the ward or to minister to the one in need. It simply creates noise that poisons the organization's culture.

President Nelson announced the retirement of the traditional visiting and home teaching programs in the April 2018 general conference of The Church of Jesus Christ of Latter-day Saints and introduced a "newer, holier approach to caring for and ministering to others. We will refer to these efforts simply as "ministering." Many new leaders have started by introducing "ministering," asking and answering questions, assessing assignments, and making sure everyone is of the same understanding. But many of us fail to start with the critical characteristic of a Relief Society or elders quorum president, which is our own ability to lead. To effectively implement this new direction that has come through inspired prophets and apostles, we can't assume that the simple waving of our metaphorical leadership arm is going to be enough to unify the Relief Society or elders quorum. We must make sure every member of our choir is focused, directed, and will adjust to whatever tempo change you make as a leader.

If this is your desire, you are reading the right book. In the following pages, you will find examples, methods, tools, and inspiration that will help you lead your ministering sisters and brothers to success!

Was Visiting and Home Teaching Really a Once-a-Month Visit Program?

Let me illustrate why leadership is so important when it comes to new programs and initiatives introduced to the Church by our leaders.

In the 1987 April General Conference, President Ezra Taft Benson gave a famous talk titled, To the Home

Teachers of the Church.

In this talk, he tells of a time as a boy when he was impacted by a visit from his home teachers.

> "I can remember, as if it were yesterday, growing up as a young boy in Whitney, Idaho. We were a farm family, and when we boys were out working in the field, I remember Father calling to us in a shrill voice from the barnyard: 'Tie up your teams, boys, and come on in. The ward teachers are here.' Regardless of what we were doing, that was the signal to assemble in the sitting room to hear the ward teachers."

> "These two faithful priesthood bearers would come each month either by foot or by horseback. We always knew they would come. I can't remember one miss. And we would have a great visit. They would stand behind a chair and talk to the family. They would go around the circle and ask each child how he or she was doing and if we were doing our duty. Sometimes Mother and Father would prime us before the ward teachers came so we would have the right answers. But it was an important time for us as a family. They always had a message, and it was always a good one."

Nice story, right?

Did you notice anything different about this story versus your personal experience?

President Benson referred to his *home teachers* as *ward teachers*. Ward Teaching was what the program was called up until 1963 when a new program was introduced called *home teaching*.

Before being known as home teachers, they were known as *ward teachers* (1912) and before that, *acting teachers*

(1909). However, for years before that time, the program was informally called *block teaching* because of the geographic way in which families were assigned (Hartley, pp. 375-98). (http://eom.byu.edu/index.php/Home Teaching)

Now, with this new announcement, we witnessed a significant adjustment to the effort to minister to others in our wards, and this time it was given the purest and most appropriate name of *Ministering.*

With the retiring of visiting and home and teaching, our leaders desire to turn our attention towards truly ministering as the Savior did. It might feel like we are now moving away from a "once a month" visiting program and starting a more sincere effort to love those we serve. However, what you might not know is that this was exactly the intent back in 1963 when the Church retired ward teaching and introduced the new home teaching program.

In 1963 it wasn't just a name change; it was to bring more emphasis to "watch over the Church" and to be concerned with the family as a whole—not a monthly visit program.

What happened after the 1963 announcement? Individuals and quorums continued old habits and focused on monthly visits. So much so that Elder James A. Cullimore of the Seventy addressed this issue in his 1972 General Conference talk. He said:

> "After nine years of home teaching, however, I am afraid we are really still doing mostly ward teaching. We are still prodding the priesthood home teachers to 'hurry and get your home teaching done—the month is nearly over.' Even now the home teacher is heard to say, 'If I really had a message to take to my families, I could do my teaching.' These things indicate we really don't have the vision of 'watching over the Church.' We might have a great record of the percentage of homes visited each month, but the

real test is: Are we affecting the lives of the individual members of the family for good through our contacts? Are we respecting the sacred nature of the family unit by working with and through the father? Do we sit down with the father as often as needed? Do we listen to him? Do we encourage and praise and otherwise uplift him?"

When Elder Cullimore gave this talk, he was concerned that the priesthood was still doing ward teaching (a monthly visit program).

And now, 46 years later, the majority of Church membership thinks we retired a "monthly visit program" in the April conference.

My point in sharing this is to focus the leader on the most challenging part of implementing the new direction to minister; which is, to lead our Relief Societies and elders quorums to what the Lord has for us today, and away from old habits and cultural norms.

Eliminating the monthly reporting ritual will definitely help, but without intentional leaders who take the time to model effective ministering, role-play scenarios, and clearly articulate expectations, we may end up in another 46 years retiring a "monthly visit program" so we can then introduce a new initiative focused on TRULY "ministering" as the Savior did.

CHAPTER 1: START WITH VISION

"*Nevertheless, the Nephites were inspired by a better cause..." (Alma 43:45).*

Captain Moroni was the greatest elders quorum president in the Book of Mormon. There is no evidence that elders quorum president was an official calling back then, but he sure did act like it. In Alma chapters 43–63 we read about the remarkable leadership skills exhibited by Captain Moroni. If studied closely, we can apply those skills to our church leadership and engage others effectively.

Here are a few examples of the impact Captain Moroni's leadership had on his armies (emphasis added):

> *"And it came to pass that when the men of Moroni saw the fierceness and the anger of the Lamanites,* ***they were about to shrink and flee from them.*** *And Moroni, perceiving their intent, sent forth and inspired their hearts with these thoughts—yea, the thoughts of their lands, their liberty, yea, their freedom from bondage." (Alma 43:48).*

*"...Moroni, on the other hand, **had been preparing the minds of the people** to be faithful unto the Lord their God."* (Alma 48:7).

*"Thus Moroni, with his armies, which did increase daily because of the **assurance of protection** which his works did bring forth unto them..." (Alma 50:12).*

Moroni engaged his armies at a higher level; they would do anything for him because he inspired them with a "better cause" (Alma 43:45). Moroni was able to perceive their intent to retreat and then motivate them to stay on task. He built assurance among his people. They knew he wouldn't let them down, and therefore they wanted to be a part of his cause.

How did he do this? How did he lead in a way that could inspire them to a level of effort that was beyond what the armies thought they could do?

There is much that Captain Moroni did to gain the love and trust of his army, but let's focus on where his success started—the Title of Liberty.

We all know the story from Primary.

After Captain Moroni had seen the evil influence Amalickiah was having on the Nephites,

*"...he rent his coat; and he took a piece thereof, and wrote upon it—**In memory of our God, our religion, and freedom, and our peace, our wives, and our children**—and he fastened it upon the end of a pole.*

And he fastened on his head-plate, and his breastplate, and his shields, and girded on his armor about his loins; and he took the pole, which had on the end thereof his rent coat, (and he called it the title of liberty) and he bowed himself to the earth, and he prayed mightily unto his God for the blessings of liberty to rest upon his brethren, so long as there should a band of Christians remain to possess the land..."(Alma 46:12–13).

> "…[Moroni] went forth among the people, waving the rent part of his garment in the air, that all might see the writing which he had written upon the rent part, and crying with a loud voice, saying
>
> Behold, whosoever will maintain this title upon the land, let them come forth in the strength of the Lord, and enter into a covenant that they will maintain their rights, and their religion, that the Lord God may bless them.
>
> And it came to pass that when Moroni had proclaimed these words, behold, the people came running together with their armor girded about their loins, rending their garments in token, or as a covenant, that they would not forsake the Lord their God; or, in other words, if they should transgress the commandments of God, or fall into transgression, and be ashamed to take upon them the name of Christ, the Lord should rend them even as they had rent their garments.
>
> Now this was the covenant which they made, and they cast their garments at the feet of Moroni, saying: We covenant with our God, that we shall be destroyed, even as our brethren in the land northward, if we shall fall into transgression; yea, he may cast us at the feet of our enemies, even as we have cast our garments at thy feet to be trodden under foot, if we shall fall into transgression." (Alma 46:19–22).

Wow!

I don't know what your experience has been, but I have never seen elders "rend their garments" and throw them at the feet of the elders quorum president as a symbol of their covenant to follow God.

This result shows the remarkable leadership of Captain Moroni!

How did he do this? He created a clear, inspiring vision that individuals wanted to follow.

I would guess that Captain Moroni established his vision long before the events described in Alma 46 because three chapters earlier, Captain Moroni refers to this vision when his soldiers' courage was tested during a battle in which they were clearly outnumbered:

> *"And it came to pass that when the men of Moroni saw the fierceness and the anger of the Lamanites,* ***they were about to shrink and flee from them.*** *And Moroni, perceiving their intent,* ***sent forth and inspired their hearts*** *with these thoughts—yea, the thoughts of their lands, their liberty, yea, their freedom from bondage.*
>
> *And it came to pass that they turned upon the Lamanites, and they cried with one voice unto the Lord their God, for their liberty and their freedom from bondage.*
>
> *And they began to stand against the Lamanites with power; and in that self same hour that they cried unto the Lord for their freedom, the Lamanites began to flee before them; and they fled even to the waters of Sidon." (Alma 43:48–50).*

I assure you that members of your Relief Society or elders quorum are thirsty for a meaningful vision and they want to go to battle for a meaningful cause. As Henry David Thoreau wrote, "The mass of men lead lives of quiet desperation." The most significant service you can give to those you lead is to provide them with a purpose that will make a difference in their community.

Without sufficiently articulating the vision of the Relief Society or elders quorum you will never win their hearts so that they do the most difficult of ministering, and you might end up unintentionally promoting a once-a-quarter visit program.

In the coming sections of this chapter, we will discuss how to effectively establish a vision for your Relief Society or elders quorum. But it is imperative to clearly state what a vision is, and what it is *not*. There have been many organizations (I'm sure you have worked for or been a part of some) that have a mission or vision statement. They pay a lot of money to have it dramatically displayed in their lobby for the world to see, but fail to have it dramatically imprinted on the hearts of their people. Captain Moroni didn't just raise the title of liberty and then put it to the side of the camp so that his army could glance at it during meal time. He referenced it and infused it into the culture of his army. When our vision begins to define our culture, that is when its potential starts to work. Let's not create visions full of ambiguous words that sound cool. Let's be specific and precise so that the culture of ministry can begin to grow.

Prepare Their Minds By Articulating the Issue

Captain Moroni was able to lead an army with strong vision because he had spent sufficient time "preparing the minds of the people." (Alma 48:7) This isn't done by dramatically ripping your best dress shirt, writing a message on it, and hoisting it to the top of a pole. There is a process to get the minds of those you lead to buy into the visionary concept so that it causes them to covenant with you and God to accomplish the vision at all costs.

"Come down" is a phrase very commonly found in the scriptures. It is often used in the context of a request to a leader—requesting they "come down" from their mountain or from whatever state they are in.

David pleaded for Saul to "come down" (1 Samuel 23:11 & 20). The Lord "came down" to the valley of Nimrod to speak with the brother of Jared (Ether 2:4). There were even times when leaders refused to "come down" because they were involved in "a great work" (Nehemiah 6:3). And, of course, "God himself should come down among the children of men." (Mosiah 34:23).

Leadership has a natural tendency to put you on a

higher level. Not in terms of pride or prestige, but instead, in terms of perspective. As a leader, you have a unique view on the status of the Relief Society or elders quorum that you lead. You have specific authority and/or priesthood keys that give you access to the inspiration that nobody else has. For example, a Relief Society president has access to ministering reports, attendance reports, etc.; she has been present in meetings, like ward council, where information about individuals or ward programs is shared.

From this exclusive information, the president might see a dramatic attendance drop between sacrament meeting and Relief Society meeting. Or, while others are doing their best to minister, the president can look at the reports and notice five specific families not getting ministering visits, which, if they did receive a visit, could have a dramatic impact on them and the ward.

Humans tend to generalize their experience or perspective. People think that because they can see a distinct issue, everyone around them can see the same issue. As a leader, we then get frustrated that this "obvious" issue isn't being recognized and fixed by others in our organization.

The leader's duty is to articulate the issue (even the "obvious" issues), so that everyone can gain a desire to find a solution. Once the issue is described and the leader invites individuals to act, those you lead will understand why this is an issue and help you find solutions.

In Abraham 3:21 the Lord "[came] down unto [Abraham] to declare unto [him]..." Abraham learned important truths of the Lord's plan and learned that he was chosen before he was born.

This was an informative experience for Abraham. He understood his purpose and took action. He could not have gained this understanding without the Lord "coming down" and articulating it to him.

I can understand if this seems frustrating. Do we need to spoon feed people so they understand the issues? Do they not see these "obvious" service gaps?

As leaders, we sometimes feel like the duty of those we lead has already been explained. We think they clearly understand the expectation to minister or magnify their calling.

It's true, there are general understandings that have been drilled into our heads for years (i.e., visit assigned families, take meals to new moms, fellowship those around you, etc.). But these are too general. It is crucial for leaders to explain detailed information about the issues that face their organization. These details usually include names of individuals struggling, or unique characteristics of your ward that may not be apparent to the armchair quarterbacks casually attending week-to-week. For example, a Sunday School president may know that he needs to keep an eye on things during the Sunday School hour, but he may not know that 20% of the ward is leaving before Sunday School begins. Or a youth leader may know he needs to put on an activity each week, but he may not realize that Brother Larsen in the elders quorum has finally made consistent contact with a less-active family with teenage boys.

Communicating from your unique leadership perspective also humanizes the issue, which makes it more likely people will be willing to help fix the issue.

A few years ago, as I was serving as a bishop, I felt a constant nudge to be more familiar with my flock. I was the bishop of a very transient ward that some months had 60 membership records leave the ward and 60 membership records come in. It was tough to keep up with who was who on the rolls. Many of these new records were for less-active families and individuals. Active ward members didn't see the reports week to week showing such a dramatic change in the ward roster. It was all happening behind the scenes, and the general ward body had no idea. As the leader of the ward, I had a unique perspective, and it was my role to "come down" and share with them what was happening. I knew I might never see a dramatic change in the ward, but I could at least know who everyone was on the rolls.

The Spirit continued to prod me. One day I printed the entire ward roster and went through each name. If I didn't recognize the name, I highlighted it. By the time I went through each name on the list I had 155 households (46% of the ward membership), and I had no idea who those people were. This was an issue. I didn't know how I was going to track down all 155 households. As a leader, I needed to take it to the ward members and invite them to act.

The following year was full of experimenting with different ideas. We tried meeting on various nights during the week (whichever was most convenient for members of the ward). We would give everyone a list of names and invite them to knock on doors and determine if the family or individual lived there, and if so, if they would attend church with us on Sunday. We made good progress, but then the winter months made it difficult to knock on doors in the evening when it was dark and cold.

We then started printing all the unknown names on a sheet of paper and handing out copies as people came into sacrament meeting. We continued this practice until I was released and all members of my ward knew they could expect an updated list each week. The bishopric took time during ward business to draw attention to the ward "find list," encouraging members to take time each week to knock on a few doors and find those sisters and brothers and who were currently lost or unknown.

The vision of "seeking out the unknown members" became part of the culture of our ward. It generated excitement and commitment because everyone knew they could make a difference by knocking on a door each week. They understood the issue, and they were regularly invited to take action from me as their bishop.

Those 155 unknown households were reduced to fewer

than 30, and we never stopped seeking out the unknown names as they were transferred into our ward.

This was not a task I could have done on my own. But because I "came down" and helped my ward understand the issues that we faced, miracles happened, and we were focused as a ward to make a difference.

Leaders too often carry the burden of the Relief Society or elders quorum issues on their shoulders, assuming everyone else sees the issue, when in fact they do not. You now must effectively communicate the identified issues to those you lead so you can take the next step of creating a vision together that inspires the Relief Society or elders quorum and creates a culture that reflects that vision.

Creating a Vision Statement

At the beginning of 2018, the Church instructed all Relief Societies and Melchizedek priesthood quorums to reformat their weekly Sunday meeting. The most significant adjustment was the monthly "council meeting" to be held the first Sunday of each month. This provided a perfect setting to discuss the purpose and vision of the quorum, but now, with the 2-hour block (announced during April 2018 general conference), Relief Society and quorum council meetings will no longer be included on the formal schedule.

With half the time to spend together as a Relief Society or quorum, leaders will need to be more creative in how they develop a quorum vision statement. Having less time should be no excuse for skipping the development of a vision statement. Remember, if you have no vision your unity will perish and these twice a month 2nd hour meetings will just turn into a single gender Sunday School class. I'd recommend you shorten the lesson plan for a few weeks until a clear vision is established.

Step 1: Introduce the Purpose of a Vision Statement

To effectively establish an individualized vision statement for your Relief Society or elders quorum you need to clearly explain (like I have done in the previous few paragraphs) why you want to create a vision statement. If you just stand up as if you are a corporate executive and say, "Today we are going to create our Relief Society (or elders quorum) vision statement," it will end up leading to a very vague activity that will produce a vague or ambiguous vision statement.

The members need to know that this vision statement will impact future activities, Sunday lessons, and every other decision or action the group makes.

It is essential to explain that this vision statement doesn't have to be a long-term vision that will last for years and years. Reflecting back on my time as a bishop when we had the vision statement to "seek out the unknown members," that vision and focus only lasted for nine to twelve months before we made considerable progress and could move on to a new vision.

If you live in a Young Single Adult ward and it is the end of the summer and you expect a large exodus and an increase of move-ins for the new school year, your vision statement for two to three months might be, "Help each new member feel at home and have an immediate circle of friends." This will be referenced in each meeting for eight to ten weeks that will influence the Relief Society or elders quorum to implement the vision.

Step 2: Create the Vision Statement with the Entire Relief Society or Elders Quorum

Many presidencies get excited about having a vision

statement and brainstorm and develop a vision statement during their presidency meeting. They then walk into their next Relief Society or elders quorum meeting and announce to the group that revelation has been received and then reveal the vision statement.

The problem with creating the vision statement during presidency meeting is that it excludes all the members of the Relief Society or elders quorum from the spiritual process of counseling together and participating in the revelatory experience. Now, this doesn't mean the presidency can't meet beforehand and develop some general ideas of where they would like the group to go and then present these ideas to get the discussion rolling.

Involving the entire Relief Society or elders quorum in this process creates buy-in—each member has a say in the direction of the group. Members are then more likely to show up to the weekly meeting and participate.

This doesn't mean the Relief Society president or elders quorum president is relinquishing her or his authority so that the organization can take control. The president should still guide the discussion. "We've talked about three different directions today, but I'm feeling prompted towards our second focus of "creating a connection with the elderly of the ward." Is anyone one else feeling the same?"

Step 3: Get Specific

The world is full of secular organizations that have a vision statement. Usually, nobody knows what that vision statement is saying. One of my favorite books on organizational communication is *Message Not Received: Why Business Communication is Broken and How to Fix It,* by Phil Simon.

In the book, he shares a quote from George Bernard Shaw, "The single biggest problem in communication is the illusion that it has taken place."

Consider this quote when developing your communication—the most significant problem you will face with creating a vision statement is ensuring that the Relief Society or elders quorum members know what it is saying. It needs to be understood and, perhaps more importantly, not misunderstood.

For example, another hilarious anecdote Phil Simon shares in his book involves Computer Sciences Corporation (CSC), an IT company based out of Virginia that later merged with HP Enterprise Services.

Before their merger, they describe themselves on their website as:

A global leader of next-generation information technology (IT) services and solutions. The company's mission is to enable superior returns on clients' technology investments through best-in-class industry solutions, domain expertise, and global scale. CSC has approximately 79,000 employees and reported revenue of $13 billion for the 12 months ended March 28, 2018.

Huh?

Maybe someone with a master's degree in Information Systems could understand what CSC is saying, but I guarantee not one of their customers has any idea what that vision statement means. The confusion that statements like this creates doesn't effectively serve as a call to battle or a statement so inspirational that people are desperate to be a part of the movement.

It became more apparent that CSC needed to fire their entire communications department when they later released this press release:

For Immediate Release: CSC Launches Next-Generation Big Data Platform as a Service FALLS CHURCH, Va., June 26, 2014—CSC (NYSE: CSC), a global leader in next-generation IT services and solutions, has added new security, compliance, data infrastructure technologies, and cloud deployment options to its open source Big Data Platform as a Service (BDPaaS) offering, which enables enterprise and public sector clients to get up and running in 30 days or less across a variety of cloud and dedicated architectures.

Come again?

There is something about human nature that prompts us to create organizational statements full of jargon and confusion even when we are trying to be as clear as possible.

When you are developing a mission statement for your Relief Society or elders quorum it might start at a high level full of Latter-day Saint jargon, but do your best to refine it down so that the newest baptized member can understand it on the first pass.

Creating a clear and straightforward vision statement has been a battle for me over the last few years. On Leading Saints you will find the vision statement: "Leading Saints is a nonprofit organization with a mission to enhance leadership ability and capacity of lay religious leaders in order to accelerate the mission of The Church of Jesus Christ of Latter-day Saints."

In general, this is a pretty straightforward mission statement, but it probably has too much of a "corporate tone". I've noticed that when I meet people and they ask me what Leading Saints does, I typically rattle off this mission statement. For clarity's sake, I've begun simply saying, "We help Latter-day Saint leaders feel prepared to lead."

When I say that simple statement, I get more dramatic positive reactions and nodding heads.

As you develop the vision statement as a Relief Society or elders quorum, do your best to remove all jargon and refine it down to the most straightforward message that someone could quickly articulate in one or two sentences.

Back in 2018 (when we had 1st Sunday council

meetings), I released a video explaining the importance of a quorum vision statement. I received an incredible email from an elders quorum president in Boise, Idaho.

He said,

Kurt,
We had our first quorum council ... I wasn't able to implement some of the tips that you sent out regarding the meeting in January... We created a quorum vision statement. I have to admit, I was a bit worried about the potential response from some of the guys in our group. Creating a vision statement is pretty outside of some of their comfort zones. I spent a fair amount of time in prayer and in council with my counselors on this topic.

I'm happy to report that it went exceptionally well. We came up with this: "We as elders in the Nampa (Idaho) 18th Ward strive to become more like the Savior by creating and responding to opportunities to strengthen ourselves, our families, our brotherhood, and our community." I'm confident we will be able to use this vision statement as a base from which we will operate in our councils to come. If it had just been my counselors and me producing a vision statement it would have likely come out much differently. I feel blessed to have done this with the entire quorum. It isn't one single person's vision or desire, but that of our entire group.

I'll attach a picture of our chalkboard. You can see a lot has been erased, ideas are on there, things have been added, and my handwriting is terrible. I think those are all signs of a successful council—minus the handwriting.

I love Leading Saints… Your resources have been absolutely invaluable to me as an elders quorum president. Maybe someday I'll be able to share some more of our progress and accomplishments with you.

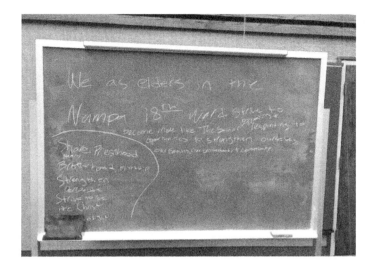

Wow! What a great email!

This good elders quorum president made it happen, and his quorum now has a vision statement that will anchor them in every action they take as a quorum.

If I were coaching him further on developing the quorum vision statement, I would probably say he could refine it to be more explicit. He could state, "We are a quorum that responds when help is needed in our ward and community."

To take it a step further, it would be helpful if the quorum had a specific focus of who or what they are responding to. If it was a YSA ward during the start of a school year, it might be, "We are a quorum that responds to every new move-in before they ask for help."

The more refined and precise your vision is, the more motivating and compelling it is to those you lead.

Vision Statements Can Take Time

At this point I hope you are excited by the potential

of what a vision statement could do for your Relief Society and elders quorum; however, as is the case with other books like this sometimes it is easier to type something on paper than implement it in the real world. Even my own experience as an elders quorum president has left me discouraged at times when trying to establish a vision or implementing other tactics shared in this book. With that said, let me give you a few items to consider that will hopefully help you avoid getting too discouraged.

As you probably already know, the time goes by fast during the last hour of church. It is sometimes possible to establish a vision statement during one Relief Society or quorum meeting, but in my experience it can take a few Relief Society or quorum meetings to get to a solid statement you can be proud of. You will find that as you introduce this idea many people in the room will need time to truly see the vision of establishing a vision. Engage the room in a way that gets individuals out of their beta state by asking them to discuss potential vision statements in smaller groups or to write down their feelings for a few minutes to help them process the question. We have unintentionally developed a culture in our Relief Society and quorum meetings where people show up, sit down, and wait to be entertained by a lesson. If you find that after one meeting you still aren't close to establishing a vision, that's okay, record what inspiration has come and then revisit it the following week. Or do you best to stimulate discussion during the meeting and then meet separately as a presidency and simplify the discussion down to one vision statement that you can introduce in the future.

The Importance of Action and Routine

There might be a lot of energy and excitement in the room when you establish a vision statement, and you will feel like you have accomplished a remarkable thing.

However, you will quickly find that as people leave the room they face a busy life full of work commitments and family responsibilities. Having a vision doesn't magically cause people to take action right away. Because of this it is crucial that you help those in your Relief Society or quorum establish simple action items that can be put into their daily routine that will cause them to engage with the vision statement.

For example, let's say you have a wonderful discussion as a group and you end us with the following vision statement, "We are a brotherhood concerned about each individual in service, love, and magnification of the gospel of Jesus Christ." You would then invite each individual into the quorum to translate that to real life, daily action items. Those might look like the following:

1. Journal daily about the following question, "Who, when, and where can I serve today?"
2. Read daily the scriptures and seek out verses related to *love*.
3. Review daily the gospel doctrines that will be discussed in our weekly quorum meeting.

It is important that you not push the same routines on each individual in the quorum. Invite them during the meeting or outside the meeting to come up with at least three daily routines that will engage them in the vision of the quorum. These should not take long to accomplish each day, maybe no longer than 10 minutes so that you don't overburden them with the routines.

This will create engagement in the vision statement and then with each ministering interview you can follow up on their daily routines related to the vision statement and note the impact the vision is having on their daily discipleship.

Building a Culture Around the Vision

Have you ever been a part of a company or organization where you almost feel a part of a movement? Like you are doing something special that is going to make a difference? If so, this probably caused you to get excited every time you went to work or showed up for a meeting. That is what good culture feels like, and good culture is the most important element a leader can develop in the Relief Society or elders quorum. I can't overstate that enough! ***Good culture is the most important element a leader can develop in the Relief Society or elders quorum.*** That's why you hear quotes like "culture eats strategy for breakfast." I would even argue that culture eats doctrine for breakfast, then it moves on to the Spirit for lunch, and then ends its day with a healthy serving of priesthood authority for dinner. I don't say that in order to say that doctrine, the Spirit, and authority are not important; rather, if you don't establish healthy culture in your Relief Society or elders quorum, nobody will ever want to take the time to join you and partake of the incredible doctrine, spirit, and priesthood authority you have.

Another fantastic quote about culture that helps us better understand how to develop it comes from Mark Templeton, former CEO of Citrix. He said,

> "The way we define culture overall is 'how [organizations] get things done.' If you have a factory, you get a lot of things done through machinery. Most companies in software get things done through people. So our machinery is people, and to put it in technology terms, people are the hardware and our values are the operating system."

The same goes for a Relief Society or elders quorum. Your machinery is people, and a healthy culture is based on how you get things done. How is the content of the meeting presented? How is the Relief Society or elders quorum meeting conducted? How effective is each ministering sister or brother? Do they know what to do? How to do it? Knowing the answers to these questions is how you "oil your machinery" (people) and how your Relief Society or elders quorum gets things done. In other words, culture!

Of course, we should work to foster a culture of love. Like Mother Teresa said, "Not all of us can do great things. But we can do small things with great love."

The reason a robust, clear vision statement is so vital is because it's the spark of culture, or the bang that starts the race. Without a vision, you have nowhere to start nor a goal to reach. Without those, you will never develop the culture that is robust enough to truly have an impact on the lives of those you lead, and all the families and individuals to whom they minister.

You can find a great example of how a vision statement or organizational purpose helps focus a culture by talking to a recently returned missionary. You could find any recently returned missionary, wake her up from a dead sleep and ask, "What is your missionary purpose?" I guarantee she will say, without missing a beat, "Invite others to come unto Christ by helping them receive the restored gospel through faith in Jesus Christ and His Atonement, repentance, baptism, receiving the gift of the Holy Ghost, and enduring to the end." (*Preach My Gospel,* Chapter 1)

This is an example of not just creating a vision statement but infusing it into the organization's culture.

Some of the best leadership advice I ever heard came from a former stake president while I was serving in a bishopric. He said during a ward conference leadership session, "Never let a quorum meeting become just another Sunday School lesson."

Sunday School is one of my favorite hours of church, and it has a focused purpose of teaching a specific curriculum that will help us learn the doctrines of the gospel. Of course, those same doctrines will come up in

Relief Society and elders quorum meetings, but those meetings should be a time for the group to share issues and concerns, discuss ideas for improvement, seek a revelatory experience, and then invite the group to take action. After counseling together, the president has authority to receive revelation for that group and should set the direction after hearing what comes out through the group revelatory council meeting. It will be helpful to hear what promptings have come to the president that will inspire group members to follow through with action.

More specifically relating to the vision statement, don't develop the mission statement and then check that box off your list. It should be a constant focal point in all of your discussions and meetings. If the meeting in a given week is focused around learning from a general conference talk about saving ordinances, it would be appropriate for the president to ask the group, "How does this doctrine or principle apply to our vision statement? How can we more deeply understand our purpose as a group by understanding this doctrine?"

Consistent reference to the vision statement will help develop a positive culture that will stimulate the execution of the vision statement. Yes, it will begin to feel redundant, or it might be easy to assume everyone gets it, and they don't need to hear it referenced over and over and over, but it's important to remind everyone why we do what we do. This reveals the higher purpose and everyone wants to be involved with a higher purpose.

Back in the days of visiting and home teaching there was a focus on monthly visits. It was typical for an elders quorum president to stand and say, "Brethren, there are only 'X' more days in the month, please make an effort to visit your home teaching families." This creates a less productive culture of focusing on making a visit once a month, and it's uninspiring.

Unfortunately, as Peter Drucker (business thought leader) has said, "What gets measured gets managed."

Reporting has shifted from monthly visits by Relief Society or elders quorum members to quarterly ministering interviews. I fear that the focus, and rote statement week-to-week will now be, "Brethren, there are only 'X' more weeks in the quarter, please get on the schedule for your ministering interview so we can hear how your families are doing." If this is the only thing repeated week-to-week or month-to-month, that will be the sign of an inferior organization culture. No matter how vital quarterly ministering interviews are, people are not inspired simply by having quarterly meetings with their leader that get checked off. They are inspired by being part of an organization that allows them to play a hand in being an answer to prayer for a family or individual through ministering.

Don't allow rote ministering interviews to be the focus of your leadership. Raise the sights of your Relief Society or elders quorum members. Lead them to a newer, holier vision everyone can get behind—actual Ministering!

CHAPTER 2: GET ORGANIZED

"It is wisdom in me; therefore, a commandment I give unto you, that ye shall organize yourselves and appoint every man his stewardship" Doctrine & Covenants 104:11

I was a single young adult desperate to find a girl who would agree to go on a date in 2005. I decided to attend the local Young Single Adult (YSA) ward in my area (swiping left or right was not an option in those days). On my first visit, I was shocked to see two elders quorums each comprised of close to 100 elders! I was more shocked a few months later when I was called as the elders quorum president of one of these very large quorums. This was my first significant leadership calling! With so many elders it felt like I was presiding over a sacrament meeting each week. Sure, I had been a deacons quorum president, teachers quorum president, and later served as a district leader to three or four companionships during my mission in Sacramento, California, but those callings never really gave me the feeling that I had a significant influence.

Like many newly called elders quorum presidents, I wanted to do a good job—I wanted to make a difference. And the way most elders quorum presidents interpreted a "good job" was an increase in the all-important key indicator, home teaching. On a newly found ego trip, I scoffed at the fact that our monthly home teaching visits were only at 40%. I, therefore, made the prideful assumption that previous administrations weren't taking home teaching seriously and I was about to bring significant change to the elders quorum as their great leader.

With little experience and riding a high of leadership pride, I didn't know what else to do but jump in and get busy working on a solution. Unfortunately, this busyness didn't include holding a presidency meeting with my counselors. And helping the elders quorum create a vision (as mentioned in Chapter 1) was the furthest strategy from my mind. I wasn't exactly sure what to do with my counselors, so I started working on a solution by myself. This led to very late nights in the clerk's office analyzing home teaching routes, as if that was what inspiring leadership looked like—staring at a screen and clicking a computer mouse. As in most YSA wards, there was a lot of turnover with young adults coming and going during their busy lives. I felt the most significant issue was to get home teaching routes assigned just right, as if there was a secret formula God challenged me to find for visits to shoot up to 100%. I was making the assumption that the motivation to home teach was directly tied to organizing the home teaching routes just right.

After several hours on multiple days of several weeks in the clerk's office working on getting the home teaching assignments just right, I printed them out and had them ready to distribute a good ten days before the next reporting month began. I was also prepared with a thick book of postage stamps I was going to use to mail out assignments to those who didn't attend elders quorum that Sunday so that they would have *no excuse* of depriving their assigned households of a visit.

And for good measure, I gave the elders quorum an

old-fashioned home teaching lesson that was dripping in guilt trips and shame. Let's just say I was exhausted after this extensive exercise and dreaded the next month when I would have to continue the home teaching organizing marathon for another set of new move-ins while considering all the move-outs.

It probably comes as no surprise that the next month there was not an increase in that 40% visit number. In fact, it decreased to 39%! I felt defeated and humbled as this trend continued for the remaining time of my elders quorum service. I had increased respect for those previous elders quorum presidents whom I thought earlier were not taking this seriously.

The Calling Monster

What I experienced as a young elders quorum president is similar to what other young, rookie leaders experience. There is a general desire to be a great leader and to be the catalyst for positive change. This usually leads to putting in more and more hours and delegating less and less. In any leadership calling an individual will face what I have named the *Calling Monster*.

The *Calling Monster* is hungry and is never satisfied. It nags you so that you can't fall asleep and wakes you up when you do. It shows up at your workplace reminding you there is more to do in your calling. This monster desperately wants you to feed it even more than feeding your children. What does the *Calling Monster* feed on?

Time, and lots of it.

I never realized the *Calling Monster* was there as a young elders quorum president, but a few years later when I was called as a bishop, I realized this beast had always been there begging me for another hour of my time it could devour. My demanding bishop's schedule made my previous elders quorum president demands look rather rudimentary. The *Calling Monster* was pulling me away from my family, my work, and my personal responsibilities, I realized that if I wanted to be a bishop for 40 hours a week, I wouldn't run out of things to do. Even 80 hours a week could be filled with "bishoping" tasks. I often found myself at work hiding in an empty conference room with the lights out and my cell phone to my ear trying to untangle the latest ward drama or a personal crisis in the life of a member. Or I would be racing to the ward building on a random night of the week feeling like it was my duty, and mine alone, to rush to any spiritual or temporal fire and give my best effort to put it out.

A year or so into my calling as an exhausted bishop I realized that just like when I was an elders quorum president, my time was being devoured by the *Calling Monster*. He was causing me to be a reactionary, administrative leader rather than a warm, measured leader who had time to offer love and support to those who desperately needed it. I was doing things the executive secretary, ward clerk, or bishopric counselors could easily do. These were typically little things that "would only take a few minutes"—but those minutes turned into HOURS! During this time, I reflected on memories from my youth when my ward and youth leaders seemed to have all the time in the world for me. There was never a rushed handshake as they raced to their next meeting. They took the time to show interest in me through sincere questions about how my life was going, how I was performing in school, and talk about relationships and life trials that often made it difficult being a teenager. Now, a decade later I realized I wanted to be *that* kind of leader.

I soon named this ideal leadership persona: *Bishop Smiley*. It became my goal to be Bishop Smiley every time I was acting in this sacred leadership role. I instructed my counselors that we needed to make it our goal to free up my time so that those we led felt their bishop had time for them and was consistently serving as Christ would serve. It was the bishopric counselors' job, along with other auxiliary presidencies, to be the spiritual firefighters in the ward as best they could while I ministered as Bishop Smiley. I informed the ward council that Bishop Smiley's role was to be the measured leader who takes the time to shake hands and look into the eyes of each member and to let them know I had all the time in the world to listen and be present. Bishop Smiley doesn't scramble to find a substitute for the Sunday School class that has a missing teacher. There is no time for Bishop Smiley to hurry to the chapel on a weeknight he isn't scheduled to be there because Bishop Smiley is at home, being Father Smiley to his children. Being Bishop Smiley (or President Smiley) is less about putting in service hours and more about often saying *no* so that you have the time and energy to lead and love.

To begin your efforts in organizing your Relief Society or elders quorum ministering it is important to realize you too have a *Calling Monster* standing by anxiously waiting to devour your time. My invitation to those Relief Society and elders quorum presidents is to commit to being President Smiley. Be intentional in your plan and spread the wealth of responsibilities. This is the best defense against any *Calling Monster* you face who is hungry for your next minute so he can devour your next hour. Instead of asking "what would Jesus do?" start asking "what would Jesus NOT do?" Christ never hurried from place to place with the intent of healing every blind person in Jerusalem; we know this because if he did there would have never been a beggar outside the temple (Acts 3) for Peter and John to heal, which gave them the opportunity to grow as leaders.

Delegate, Delegate, Delegate

Ask any experienced leader for advice, and very likely they will tell you to "DELEGATE!" But delegation in practice is much more difficult than one might expect. When it comes to ministering, I strongly emphasize that the Relief Society or elders quorum president delegate ALL administrative tasks associated with ministering. (Note that I said administrative tasks, NOT Bishop Smiley tasks! More on this later.) I have seen too many presidents (like my younger self) spend hours thinking they have to have administrative oversight regarding who is assigned where and when and to whom. I have seen too many complicated spreadsheets developed by ambitious Relief Society or elders quorum presidents who can't stop tweaking it month to month. Delegate it! Pick a counselor and delegate the keys to this responsibility. Don't ask leaders to organize the list and then lurk over their shoulder making suggestions at each decision; give them clear direction, "I need you to make sure everyone in our Relief Society has a ministering assignment and that every sister has ministering sisters assigned to her."

If your counselors are too overwhelmed by this assignment, it usually means they need help establishing a better system. The assignment shouldn't be too difficult or time-consuming. The May 11, 2018 FAQ addendum notes that the callings of ministering coordinator and ministering supervisor (previously known as home or visiting teaching coordinators) have been discontinued. The new FAQ highlights that ministering secretaries can be called to support the presidency. A temporary, small committee could be called to get the process up and running. Again, I doubt this will be necessary with the right systems in place.

I promise you there is no chalkboard in heaven where God has written down the exact ministering assignments for your Relief Society or elders quorum and it is up to you to match it exactly. It is your job as president to use your intelligence and life experience, your counselors' feedback, and your inspiration to make the best assignments you can. There is no optimum combination that leads to perfect ministering success. Delegate this responsibility and when it is done look it over with the help of the bishop and then move on. There might be a few adjustments you will recommend, but your counselor or secretary can handle the tweaking so you can focus on more important work.

What is that more important work? I will discuss this more in the Ministering Interviews chapter, but the primary focus of the Relief Society and elders quorum president should be ministering interviews. These interviews are where President Smiley thrives and makes the most difference in the hearts of those he or she leads. In fact, I will explain in the Ministering Interviews chapter why it is critical that the Relief Society and elders quorum president personally conduct each one of those ministering interviews. I know… I know… you think I am talking crazy to suggest that the Relief Society or elders quorum president conduct every single ministering interview, but I will soon explain why your purpose "numero uno" has to be this critical one-to-two (preferred) or one-to-one interview. BUT to make that happen, you must remove ALL administrative tasks from your to-do list. Delegate them and be President Smiley.

In short, the most effective weapon against the *Calling Monster* is building effective and efficient administration systems so you can focus on ministering. Delegation isn't about giving a task or assignment to someone else, so you don't have to do it. Delegation is about giving tasks to established systems that do all the thinking with your counselor (or any individual) monitoring the system. Paul Gustavson, a well-respected business consultant, former YSA bishop, and author of *Team of Leaders* has said, "teams are perfectly designed to get the results that they get."

For example, when someone moves into the ward and needs to be brought up to speed with the goals of the Relief Society or elders quorum and receive a ministering assignment, there should be a four-step (or six-step or whatever-step) procedure that helps new members easily learn what they should do. Establish as many procedures and administrative systems as possible and your team of leaders will be less likely to burn out.

Make It Easy

Now that we have clearly stated the importance of delegating the administrative tasks of ministering, let's talk about some ideas and approaches the Relief Society, or elders quorum president could suggest to their presidency to get this done. It would be entirely appropriate, especially when a new presidency has been called, to use time in the Sunday third hour to talk about ministering assignments. Ministering is already happening in your Relief Society or elders quorum—you might as well leverage those organic ministering efforts rather than giving members new, arbitrary assignments.

For example, let's say Brother Spendlove recently moved into a new ward knowing very few people. After a few weeks, he meets Brother Borland who has the same love for fishing he does. They set up a time to take the boat to the lake, and this sparks a friendship where they regularly visit different fishing spots while having conversations about life. In this scenario, there is nobody else in the ward more qualified to be Brother Spendlove's ministering brother than Brother Borland (or vice-versa). A relationship is already established and ministering is already happening since Brother Spendlove would not hesitate to call Brother Borland in a time of need or support.

There are other types of organic relationships, that, if identified, could make the Relief Society or elders quorum ministering efforts easier. Let me share with you three different ways to identify organic ministering that is already happening.

Existing Friendships

The Brother Spendlove/Borland scenario is an

example of this. Most members of your ward will have established friendships that could become ministering assignments. Not everyone can be matched to their best ward friend, but I am sure many can to make ministering easier and more sincere.

Take time in Relief Society or elders quorum, or even in a ministering interview, to learn who each person is a close friend with in the ward, or other "casual friends" with whom they already associate. You could survey Relief Society or elders quorum members and ask them who their friends are. One tactic I used in a recent elders quorum meeting was to pass around a simple questionnaire with one of the questions being, "If you were at the airport at 4 am and needed a ride home and could only call someone in the ward (other than a family member) who would you call?" Or you could use the question, "If you needed a priesthood blessing in the middle of the night who in the ward would you call?"

Questions like these give greater insight—you may not get a straight answer if you randomly asked someone, "Who is your best friend in the ward?" Framing the question in the context of ministering activities will likely bring to mind a member's existing organic ministering relationships.

Callings

Another way to identify an established relationship in the ward is by considering an individual's church calling. I remember team teaching the 14-year-old Sunday School class with a brother I wasn't familiar with when we were first called. A few months in I considered him a good friend and would have had no problem contacting him in a time of need. Or consider a Primary presidency that meets each week to visit the homes of Primary children—there are many conversations about life happening while driving to the next house. Most presidencies are BFFs by the time they serve together for a few months. When individuals serving in a calling together are asked to take it to the next level by ministering to one another, it creates a deeper bond that will help them succeed in their calling because they are more likely to find ways outside of the calling to serve one another.

Propinquity

Imagine you are taking your daily walk out to the mailbox to see the bills and advertisements with which you have been blessed when you look across the street and see your neighbor, Brother Ben Brandt, kneeling on the ground sweating over his lawnmower. You give him a wave, and after acquiring your stack of mail, you take a moment to walk across the street to touch base as a friendly neighbor.

"Hey, Ben! What's new?" you say.

Alerted by your greeting Ben says, "Oh, hi! Just trying to take advantage of this nice weather to cut my lawn. It would be a lot easier if I could get this thing started."

"What seems to be the problem?" you reply.

"I'm guessing it's the carburetor, but I am fresh out of carburetor cleaner," Ben says.

With friendly excitement you say, "I had the same problem last week and picked up some carburetor spray at the hardware store. Let me go grab it and let's give it a spray."

You jog back to your garage, grab the spray and return in less than a minute.

"Here you go! Give that a try."

Ben smiles as he finally gets the engine to turn over. You return home after receiving a thankful handshake.

Do you know what just happened? Ministering! It was no big deal, but it sure made a difference in Ben's life and got him moving forward; however, Ben probably didn't think to call his ministering brothers just to get his lawnmower started. Maybe he should have, but most people don't want to create a fuss over things unless they are in dire need.

This is the magic of propinquity! Propinquity is "the state of being close to someone or something; proximity." One of the biggest hurdles in being an effective ministering sister or brother is proximity; especially when you are outside of Utah and you are geographically dispersed. No matter how many phone calls or emails you may send to the families you minister to, things are much easier when you are a short walk or short drive away. You also have a higher chance of stumbling upon an opportunity of service or being close enough to observe the everyday activities of your families so you can notice when things are out of the ordinary.

Being mindful of your ward geographics can significantly help accomplish your Relief Society or elders quorum ministering goals. Let's dive deeper into this concept by talking about the power of districts.

Districts

Do you remember back in Chapter 1 when I shared the story about when my ward sought out the unknown names on our ward roster? One useful tactic we used: create districts. Our bishopric pulled up our ward boundaries on Google Maps and worked together to draw districts within our ward boundaries (you can find your ward boundaries at maps.ChurchofJesusChrist.org, and you can see how to draw on Google Maps on YouTube). Then we were able to see how many unknown names were in each district and ask active members in that district to make some time to knock on the doors of unknowns and determine what their status was. Organizing in this way made it easier to keep track of the unknowns and also made the task easier for active members since they only had to walk a few doors down (or drive a few blocks) to accomplish the assignment. This is how you leverage the power of propinquity.

When making ministering assignments, enable the Relief Society or elders quorum members to also act as a ministering brother or sister to those households in their district. Though members of your Relief Society or elders quorum may already have assigned ministering families, there is no reason why a Relief Society or elders quorum president couldn't ask them, during each ministering interview, about the families that live near them. This could provide a report on any observations they have made just by living close to others.

Once you get your Relief Society or elders quorum organized into districts, there are so many other ways you can leverage them. You might have thought district leaders and visiting teaching supervisors were a thing of the past. Though we may now call them district leaders or any other name you like (and they won't be collecting monthly reporting numbers), you can still use them in a variety of ways. For example, in November 2017, before the retirement of the home teaching program, I interviewed Matthew Stevens, an elders quorum president in Colorado, USA. He called district leaders as did many elders quorum presidents at that time, but he saw a higher purpose for these districts. He used them to delegate specific elders responsibilities as they arose. If there were a new move-in happening, he would ask District 2 to organize and help that new family move in. New welfare assignment down at the church cannery? District 4 was sent this time to fulfill that assignment. Now that elders quorums are in charge of temple and family history you could make District 1 the new Temple and Family History Committee. The district leader would then report to one of the counselors in the elders quorum presidency. If a new family moves into the ward, the counselor assigned to organize assignments could look at which district the new family is in and assign them to a ministering companionship living in the same district, increasing the chance of effective ministering because you are leveraging the power of propinquity. The work moves forward with an organized delegation system built on districts (which are geographically based).

Not all assignments will perfectly fit into each one of these approaches, but hopefully, you can use these tactics and find your own, to make ministering easier for those who sincerely want to minister.

Stop Ministering to the Bishop

I once heard someone say that the bishop of the ward deserves the best-of-the-best ministering brothers because he is carrying most of the workload and needs the most support. I understand why this might be a good idea, but the bishop is also the only person in the ward who, if he stopped coming to church, would be noticed by everyone! His obligations might wear him out, but these responsibilities at least keep him engaged in the gospel. Though it makes a catchy heading in a book, I am not suggesting that we avoid ministering to the bishop, but we should be intentional about making sure those in the most need are assigned first. In my experience, most wards first assign ministering sisters and brothers to the most active people in the ward. By the time they get to the less-active, there aren't many ministering sisters or brothers to go around. In Doctrine & Covenants 81:5 we are given the charge "to stand in the office which I have appointed unto you; succor the weak, lift up the hands which hang down and strengthen the feeble knees." So why are we succoring the strong, lifting up hands already raised, and helping healthy knees? Yes, of course, it might be that those who appear the strongest are actually the weakest, but there is a better way to seek out the feeble knees.

Consider the approach of an elders quorum president from South Carolina, USA. He served during the time of home teaching and one day while he reviewed the handbook he noticed the phrase, "Quorum leaders …assign the most effective home teachers to members who need them most." He studied the home teaching assignments and wasn't sure those with the most need were getting the best or most consistent home teachers. He decided to take a new approach, and it started with a spreadsheet. He exported the ward list into a spreadsheet (which leaders can do through the online ward directory). He created additional columns according to the Handbook 2 guidance for which households should be assigned first: new members, less-active members, single parents, widows, and widowers. He put each category as a column heading and considered other circumstances in his ward where a household would benefit from good home teachers. Then, going name by name, he checked all the boxes that applied to each name. If they were single they got a checkmark; if they were in poor health, they got another checkmark. Once each name was considered he was able to sort the spreadsheet according to the households that had the most checkmarks and assign home teachers (now ministering brothers) accordingly. He ran the risk of some very active members not receiving much attention, but it prioritized his flock in a way that was helping those most in need.

Note that in the new ministering effort more households (on average) could be assigned to a companionship than was possible in the home teaching program since we are not being measured by a formal monthly in-person visit. The average ward could easily assign ministering sisters and brothers to each household, and these ministering sisters and brothers do their best to minister—by texts, emails, social media contacts, or in-person visits.

Organizing & Scheduling Ministering Interviews

In the next chapter we will discuss some best practices

related to conducting ministering interviews, but before we can hold interviews, we must first organize and schedule them. As we learned in the April 2018 general conference, the only ministering measurement that will be reported to the Church are quarterly ministering interviews conducted by the Relief Society or elders quorum presidency. For most Relief Societies or elders quorums, this should be a simple task as long as it has a scheduled cadence.

With this increased emphasis on ministering interviews, the Relief Society and elders quorum secretary are going to feel more and more like the bishop's executive secretary—managing appointments and calendars. It is definitely within the rights of the president to call additional assistant secretaries to help with this workload, but with the right use of tools, it should be manageable with one secretary in most Relief Societies or elders quorums.

Tools

Let's run through some tools and applications available to Relief Society and elders quorum presidencies that will streamline the workload. If there are any tools that you have found helpful that are not listed below, please share them with us at LeadingSaints.org/contact so that we can add them to the list in future editions.

Google Calendar

Google Calendar has been around for quite a few years, and I would assume the general audience of this book is familiar with this app and is most likely already using it. Whether you use Google Calendar or another free calendaring system, it is essential to have a calendar you can sync to as a presidency, so everyone's schedule is known. It saves a lot of back-and-forths when you are all looking at the same calendar. If you are unfamiliar with this tool, you can find easy-to-follow tutorials with a quick search for Google Calendar on Youtube.com.

For example, the Relief Society or elders quorum president could tell the secretary that ministering interview time is available each week after church for two hours. The secretary can then make contact with ministering sisters or brothers and schedule appointments within the allotted time. The Relief Society or elders quorum president will see appointments immediately sync up with their Google calendar.

Scheduling Services

A scheduling service is an online application that allows individuals to get on your schedule through a simple link. After clicking the link, they are taken to a webpage that shows a list of appointment options all based on your availability so that they can only schedule an appointment within a timeframe you have chosen to conduct ministering interviews. The service we use at Leading Saints for our scheduling is Acuity Scheduling, and it would work perfectly for scheduling ministering interviews.

There is a free option, but if you want your appointments to sync with your Google calendar, there is a minimal cost. The bishop, Relief Society president, and elders quorum president might want to consider a paid option if they all like the service and it fits in the Administration budget.

ChurchofJesusChrist.org Email Blasts

With an ever-changing Relief Society or Elders quorum roster, it becomes difficult to keep your email list up to date. However, if you log in to Leader and Clerk Resources (LCR) on ChurchofJesusChrist.org, there is an option to send a mass email out to all those in your Relief Society or Elders quorum who have an email listed in their membership records. You can find the "Send a Message" option under the "Applications" menu in LCR.

Member Tools Map Function

This is one of my favorite functions in the Member Tools smartphone app. As a leader, you are given additional functionality through the Member Tools app. By clicking on the Reports option on the main menu and then Unit Statistics, you can see different demographics for your ward. If you then click on "Women" it will show you a list of all the adult women in your ward (the same applies for "Men"). You can then click the map icon in the top right corner, and it will display all these names on a map according to where they live. This is a great reference as your secretary is scheduling appointments so that you can group individuals in the same area so you can visit them in their home or so they don't have to travel as far to meet up with you if you desire to do these interviews in person. This is also a great tool to reference while making ministering assignments so you can easily see who lives near each other.

I love to use this function when I am out visiting someone in my elders quorum—I can quickly see who lives nearby and pop in and say hello.

Video Conferencing Apps

It's great to know that ministering interviews do not have to be conducted in person. Doing them in person is preferred and allows you to connect with individuals more effectively (more to come on this in the next chapter). An alternative to in-person meetings is face-to-face video conferencing. Learning to use a video conferencing app can save you travel time or enable you to meet with someone where your schedules don't sync for an in-person interview.

The most widely used video conferencing app is Skype, which is easy to download on a computer that has access to a camera and microphone. Skype also has an easy-to-use smartphone app you can download through Apple or Android.

Facetime is also very popular if both parties are using an Apple device.

Ministering Interviews Appointment Management

If the Relief Society or elders quorum president does commit to doing ministering interviews in person, it might be tempting to have the Relief Society, or elders quorum secretary put together a sign-up sheet with dates and times that will be passed around during the third-hour meeting inviting people to sign up for their ministering interview. I'll save my rant about my detestation for signup sheets for another book, but your secretary's effort to schedule interviews doesn't have to be that complicated. I assume many elders quorum presidencies will assign their secretary to develop a schedule with set times for interviews and then invite each member of the Relief Society or quorum to schedule a time slot for the appointment. This will lead to the secretary communicating a complicated schedule to whomever is doing the interview and then if you get behind schedule it starts a domino effect that you are late to multiple appointments and then you will try to keep appointments short and you will seem rushed, and on and on and on.

This is why I recommend the "Cable Guy Strategy." Here's how it works… You divide up your ward boundaries into districts (my elders quorum has 5 districts). Each week the secretary sends out an email to all individuals in a specific district, notifying them that the ministering interview will happen between a set time (i.e.

between 1 pm and 3 pm on Sunday). The presidency member then starts knocking doors during that time period in that specific district. There is no hard appointment schedule to stay on top of and everyone you are visiting is expecting you to show up. This has worked miracles in my quorum! I am able to see several individuals each week and I am never rushing from one visit to the next. If my time runs out, those elders I didn't see know that I will try them the next time I am in the area. If they have a commitment or get tired of waiting, that's okay, I simply try them back the next time I'm in the area. So handle it like the cable guy, give them a range of time when you will be stopping by and it simplifies the process.

Scheduling ministering interviews right after church at the church building might be the only option for in-person interviews if the ward is geographically spread out. However, if your ward boundaries are smaller (Utah), you might have more success going to each ministering sister or brother and meeting with them in their home. This can be done by using the "cable guy strategy", and you will be surprised how much more willing people will be to schedule a ministering interview if the interview is coming to them.

Only the President

As mentioned earlier in this chapter, having the president of the Relief Society or elders quorum be the only one who conducts ministering interview might be a controversial idea. Every time I mention it to a Relief Society or elders quorum leader I get a face of skepticism. But hear me out, and at the beginning of the next chapter, I am going to share an example with you that will hopefully win you over to this opinion.

Wait a second! It's completely appropriate to have presidency counselors conduct interviews. Why put all the burden on the president?!?!

Remember: Delegation is critical to avoid the *Calling Monster* who will eat up every last minute you give it! So now we have to identify the administrative and ministering tasks that MUST be delegated to others, and the one task that MUST NOT be delegated.

Organizing weekly Relief Society or elders quorum lessons should be handled by a counselor. Ministering assignments in the computer system should be made by a counselor or secretary. Do you have a welfare assignment down at the cannery? A counselor should handle it. Is the elders quorum in charge of the upcoming chili cook-off? Yep, a counselor can handle that too. If there is too much to do for the two counselors, call a committee to help out.

Every responsibility should be delegated to counselors or the secretary EXCEPT FOR THE MINISTERING INTERVIEWS! I can't emphasize this enough. If the ministering interviews take up 90% of the Relief Society or elders quorum presidents' time, it will lead to a more motivated group, a more committed group, and most importantly a more unified group.

The story behind how I arrived at this conclusion is a perfect introduction to the next chapter. So turn the page and let's talk about Ministering Interviews.

CHAPTER 3: MINISTERING INTERVIEWS

"We don't count, but we 'render an account.'" — Elder Gary E. Stevenson (see D&C 72:3)

A year after being married, and after what I felt was a failed attempt at being a stand-out elders quorum president, my wife and I moved out of the world's smallest basement apartment and into a condo that felt like a royal mansion. Our new condo was within the boundaries of the Lee Ward, and we were excited to serve. Only a few months after moving in that opportunity to serve was thrown at us—in an intense way. At the age of 25, I was called into the bishopric to serve alongside an incredible bishop who became a great mentor. That experience lasted just under two years when it was time for the bishop to be released. According to tradition and handbook direction, I was called in to meet with a counselor in the stake presidency. I was not surprised with the release from the bishopric but was surprised to hear that the stake presidency had a new calling for me, high priest group leader. I was 26 years old at the time, and I thought that calling was for those over the age of 50. With my wife by my side, I gladly accepted the calling and looked forward to getting started.

A few weeks later it felt strange standing in front of 15 or so high priests in a group meeting. The majority of them were old enough to be my father, and I could sense their confusion why a young buck had been called to be their "leader." Because of my disheartening attempt at being an elders quorum president a few years before, I still had feelings of inadequacy. I wanted to succeed as a high priest group leader as much as I had as an elders quorum president. Would my attempt fall flat once again?

As I jumped back into organizing home teaching assignments I was more open to delegating to my leadership team. With fewer members of the group compared to the elders quorum I previously presided over it took much less time to get home teaching organized. The home teaching report was much more encouraging among those high priests—it had been consistently around 60–70%. However, I felt stuck as a leader because I still didn't know what to do to find more success or how to move the group forward.

I don't entirely remember where the idea originated from, but I do remember my stake president made a strong emphasis on regular home teaching interviews where a member of the ward's high priest group leadership would meet regularly with each companionship. I liked hearing this because it gave me something on which I could focus. I decided that I would make this my entire focus and do it on a regular monthly basis. The high priest group secretary filled up my Wednesday evenings with a handful of 15-minute appointments with several high priests in the group. Each Wednesday evening my presidency would meet at the centrally located condominium clubhouse, have a brief presidency meeting, and then my two assistants would go out visiting members of the ward while I stayed at the clubhouse in the common area and interviewed each high priest on my schedule for that night.

The best way to describe these interviews, in the beginning, is "awkward!" Here I was a 26-year-old returned missionary sitting down with 50-plus-year-old established priesthood holders asking them about their personal gospel experience and their home teaching efforts. I also didn't have much of an interview agenda to follow, so the conversations seemed superficial and, again, awkward. But I stuck with it, meeting at least once each month with each member of my group. I slowly developed a simple 10-minute agenda where I would address home teaching progress, but much of the time I was getting to know each of them as an individual and touch on topics that would invite the Spirit into our discussion. Over time I sensed a shift in these interviews. These men 20-to-30 years my senior were becoming my friends. Many of them began opening up to me. About the struggles they faced in life. The difficulties of being an older divorcee in the church. The broken relationships with their children they desperately wanted to repair. Being out of work. And even not holding a temple recommend when they desired so much to get back on track spiritually. These were incredible interactions I began to look forward to each month.

Of course, there were a few personalities in the group that never really embraced these regular meetups, and those remained a little awkward, but the vast majority turned into a deep connection between me, their priesthood leader, and each member of the group.

After a few months, I not only noticed a deeper connection forming but additional changes began to happen as a result of these consistent interviews. Sunday group meetings had a greater feeling of unity and a positive group culture because I had established a relationship with each one. Each felt their high priest group leader knew them personally and therefore they all wanted to know each other personally.

Then I looked at the home teaching percentages after a few months, and I was shocked to see it had increased by at least 20% and we consistently stayed in the high 90% range for the two years I was in that calling. I have no doubt this was due to the consistent, monthly interviews where each brother knew he would be sitting down with his priesthood leader and be asked to "render an account" of his efforts. Accountability is a great motivator when encouraging others to engage in the work.

By the time I was released as the high priest group leader I had such a sweet relationship with these "older" brothers that many of these relationships continue today. My release came when I received the call to serve as bishop of the ward. These high priests treated me like a graduating grandson who was moving on. They were excited to support me as their bishop, and it was refreshing to have a high priest group that I could rely on in my new capacity.

Consistency is Key

As I have interacted with Relief Society and elders quorum presidents in my stake and in the Leading Saints community the number one piece of advice I have offered is to have consistent *one by one* interviews with each member of the Relief Society or quorum, which includes the president being the one consistently present in these interviews. As Elder Ballard emphasized in the recent ministering training, we should emulate the Savior's actions as reported in 3 Nephi 18:36 when "he touched… the [ministers] whom he had chosen, *one by one*…" (Although the scripture refers to the physical touch of the Savior, we can also consider this as being touched by the Spirit in our ministering interviews.) You can imagine my excitement when I heard in general conference that these personal interviews will now be the key metric reported and tracked by the Church. The driving force of making ministering interviews overwhelmingly valuable is consistency. Consistency when they are held. Consistency in who conducts the interview (the quorum president). And finally consistency of how the interviews are conducted.

At this point, a Relief Society or elders quorum president might be overwhelmed with the idea of trying to do so many *one by one* interviews, and you don't see why you can't just rotate this responsibility with your counselors. The manner in which you approach these interviews is entirely up to you and should be a prayerful decision, but let me summarize with you three key reasons the president of the Relief Society or quorum will find greater success by personally conducting each ministering interview.

Relationship

During my full-time mission in Sacramento, California, USA, I had the opportunity to serve with two mission presidents, President Robert Grow, and President Craig Hansen. Every six weeks, like most missionaries in the Church, I sat down with my mission president *one by one* to render an account. Mission presidents have two counselors, but I assume they are not permitted to divide up the interview responsibilities among their counselors, and that's a blessing! Can you imagine meeting with a different member of the mission presidency every time? Would missionaries have the same personal relationship with their mission president or would it feel more like an administrative exercise not focused on relationships? The relationship between the missionary and the mission president is crucial when it comes to getting the work done and helping missionaries stay engaged. Most returned missionaries reading this love and respect their mission president and would probably do anything he asked them to do, even if he called today with a request. This loyalty is due to the relationship built, primarily through these *one by one* interviews.

Many reading this have probably worked for an organization where the CEO or leader of the company feels distant. The leader becomes a caricature figure who barks out orders through email or mandates general policy. This results in gossiping around the water cooler because each person feels that the leader is just a bureaucratic head who has no understanding of their department or them as an individual. When a Relief Society or elders quorum president takes the time to know each member of their organization, it creates a natural human experience that we all crave in life—connection. When we connect we begin to see and understand each other for who we are, and when we know each other, we want to serve each other. Building individual relationships will instill a culture of ministering, and you will find everything gets easier. Invitations to serve at the upcoming welfare assignment will more likely be accepted. Mutual respect during Sunday meetings will increase when you speak because you know each one personally. Even consistent attendance will go up because members no longer feel invisible in the back of the room.

I am beyond grateful for the relationships I built by taking the time to interview those in my high priest group long ago. I remember one brother in particular who I first met as his high priest group leader. When I was called as bishop, he often told me that he struggled for years to attend church regularly, but that it had become much more comfortable now that I was his bishop. Every time he would walk into the chapel he would always look towards the stand and make eye contact with me. He would give me a nod and a slight smile. This connection got him out of bed on Sunday mornings because he knew his bishop knew him, loved him, and wanted to see him there. I even had a phone call with this good brother a few weeks ago, years after our high priest group experience. He still sees me as a leader because he sees me as a friend.

Accountability

We learn a remarkable leadership principle each time we attend the temple. When you give an assignment, pair it with the request to return and report. When ministering interviews are consistently given solely by the Relief Society or quorum president, expectations can be clarified, and there is less chance of returning with a vague report to a presidency counselor who wasn't sure what was expected in the first place.

Accountability done incorrectly will leave members of your Relief Society or quorum less likely to follow you as their leader. During the years of visiting and home teaching we probably all lived in a ward at one time where a phone call (or worse, a text message) would come through with a simple query, "Brother Hulsberg, did you get your home teaching done?" It's to the point, direct, and I guess it helped the presidency get closer to a completed report, but accountability, especially in the gospel, is so much more. When a leader asks a question of accountability, it can't be done with an inward intention as if they are only asking to fill out their report. It must be an outward expression of not only asking if the ministering is being done but if the ministering is accomplishing the vision of the Relief Society or quorum, which in turn is changing each one as an individual and helping them reach their personal goals. That type of request cannot be done without a consistent interview with the president who is getting to know them on a deeper level.

Engagement

If there is one indicator that is most related to the success of any Relief Society or quorum it would be engagement. Gallup, an American based research company, has done countless studies on engagement (*State of American Workplace Report*, Gallup) in the workplace and the results are always staggering. Typically, they find that most people are 33% engaged on the job. So if you have 100 people working in your office it's as if you only have 33 people, on average, working at full force. There have been no engagement studies in the Latter-day Saint group setting, but I suspect that engagement is much lower. Not because members of the church are less valiant in their church efforts compared to their work efforts, but because they have not been given enough purpose to foster engagement (and they aren't given a paycheck for their efforts).

The exercise of sitting down with a member of your Relief Society or quorum allows you to measure their engagement and have a real conversation about it. Imagine the power of these ministering interviews if you connect with each individual on a personal level so that they feel comfortable bringing up the biggest reason why they might be disengaging from the Relief Society or quorum experience. This happened to me as bishop when I was frustrated by the lack of discussion that was happening in our ward council meetings. I felt like I would present very poignant topics related to the ward and then everyone would blink at me in silence. One Sunday as I was meeting with the ward elders quorum president I asked him about this. He told me that he never spoke up because he only had a few seconds to consider the topic I was presenting. As the bishop, I had the entire previous week to ponder the topic, and I was only giving my ward council a few seconds to process the same information.

Because of this interview, I began sending the topic and related resources to the ward council several days before our meeting so they would be prepared to participate. This information and adjustment all came from the regular *one by one* interview with my elders quorum president. These interactions built a relationship where he was comfortable enough to tell me the problem from his viewpoint. Imagine how valuable it would be to find out a member of your Relief Society is too shy to approach assigned ministering sisters or she is having a difficult time ministering sincerely to her assigned sisters. You can then address it together, come up with some action items and, in turn, re-engage her *one by one* in the Relief Society vision statement.

But what about…?

From my personal experience, I have seen miracles come from putting my entire focus as a quorum president on conducting every ministering interview. It might make sense on paper, but I guarantee you will run into discouragement as you attempt to execute this plan. Before we move on to the meat of the ministering interviews, let me address a few concerns you might have.

I have so many people in my organization, how can this be done by the president alone?

If you are in an enormous Relief Society or quorum, it is going to be very easy to get discouraged when you look at the long list of individuals and wonder how you will be able to visit with each one personally. Don't fret! I promise you it can be done the same way you would eat an elephant, having processes and systems as discussed in chapter 2. The hard part is not conducting the interviews with so many people; it's scheduling and orchestrating the interviews (which should be done by the Relief Society or quorum secretary).

Take a moment to ask your bishop how he approaches tithing settlement each year. There are probably a lot of people in your ward, and he is required to attempt to meet with each household. These meetings are possible with the systems, organization, and people he has around him making it happen. Call more people to help out if needed, but again, if I had 96 elders in my quorum, I would do everything possible as their quorum president to meet quarterly with them individually (and sometimes as companionships).

Also, I can't emphasize enough the effectiveness of the "Cable Guy Strategy" I discussed in chapter 2. We have completely moved away from a complicated scheduling process and kept it simple.

Aren't we supposed to have both companionship members in the ministering interview?

Meeting with both companionship members at once is an excellent approach, but it is not required. Meeting *one by one* is appropriate and in many cases, it is the preferred option. It is going to be more difficult connecting *one by one* and sharing personal information when both ministering sisters or brothers are in the interview. Meeting with both members of the companionship also adds additional complexity to scheduling and organizing that might drive your secretary crazy. Again, it might be something worth shooting for but be sure you put excellent systems in place so you can be consistent.

Where there is a youth minister, companionship interviews may be preferred. In this case, you might have a formal interview with both of them for 10 minutes or so and then find another time to connect personally with the adult member of your Relief Society or quorum to build a meaningful relationship with them.

How can I train my counselors to do ministering interviews if I am conducting each interview? I want to make sure I am training my replacement.

Every Relief Society or quorum president should

continuously be considering how they are training their replacement. Though a presidency counselor isn't guaranteed to be your replacement when you are released, it is still the best time to get them up-close-and-personal training, so they have a general idea how to lead when their turn comes. Because of this, you should make it a habit to have a counselor (or your secretary) at each ministering interview. They might not say much because they are there primarily to observe. It will have the same feeling as a ministering visit with two individuals there ready to listen and show concern. There might be a few individuals who openly share very personal information during their interview, and you can conduct those by yourself.

I love the idea of having me as the Relief Society or quorum president do all the ministering interviews, but my group is so small that I will finish long before the quarter ends. What should I do with my time and focus until the next quarter starts?

For many, this task of personal ministering interviews will seem daunting at first, but once you get your systems in place, you will be shocked how quickly you will get through the Relief Society or quorum roster even if you have a large organization. For example, at the time of this writing, I am serving as elders quorum president in a Utah ward where we have about 65 active Melchizedek priesthood brothers in the ward who have a ministering assignment. On average I spend two hours (sometimes three) on Sunday doing ministering interviews (15 minutes each). This means I can do at least eight interviews a week and I can meet with each person in eight weeks. That leaves me with four weeks remaining in the quarter. So what do you do with the remaining time? Start over. Just like monthly home teaching visits were the minimum requirement not the maximum; quarterly ministering interviews are the "floor, not the ceiling" (though I recommend that you not do ministering interviews with the same person more than once a month). The more regularly you meet with ministering sisters and brothers, the faster you will build relationships with them and the more likely you will be able to establish a culture of ministering.

While I am busy doing all these ministering interviews when am I going to find time to do my own assigned ministering visits?

After a year or two serving as a bishop (during the time of home teaching), I requested to not be assigned a home teaching route. With the many duties of being a bishop, it became one more thing that often fell through the cracks and made me feel like I was underperforming as a bishop. I was still visiting households on a regular basis, but they were more focused visits to those families that would most benefit from a bishop visit.

Not assigning yourself a ministering route might be something to consider as a Relief Society or elders quorum president. Sure, we all want to set an example of ministering, but you will have more influence and serve the Relief Society or quorum better by ministering "*one by one.*"

I still don't understand why three members of the presidency can't rotate through the responsibility of conducting a ministering interview?

As I have stated above, I have seen significant benefit come from the president conducting each ministering interview in a personal and consistent way. However, if you don't feel moved in that direction, it is appropriate to let your counselors handle the interviews with you. If you go this route, consider creating as much consistency as possible by allowing each counselor to meet with the same individuals each time. I recommend you at least try interviewing by yourself "*one by one*." I believe you will be shocked how easy it is and, most importantly, how much you enjoy it.

Conducting Ministering Interviews

At the time of this writing, which is a few months after the announcement of the new ministering effort and the retirement of monthly reporting, many Relief Society and quorum members are excited about the fact that we no longer have to collect monthly reports from each member of the organization. Reporting on quarterly ministering interviews seems so much sincerer and doable, so we are excited to jump in.

The first interview or two will be great! Everyone is excited about this new approach to serving individual families in their ward and are willing to help out. They will likely express some excitement about being assigned to specific families and assure you, their Relief Society or quorum president, that they will take a proactive approach to help those families feel loved and supported in the ward. The next time you meet with them in a ministering interview, they may express some unexpected circumstances that haven't allowed them to serve as they would want but they will be committed to making some adjustments and seeing progress. Then, after a few interviews, as these ministering interviews begin to feel more routine, you may start to see a natural apathy settle in that you recognize from the days of visiting and home teaching. Instead of receiving upbeat commitment you might not get more than a shrug of discouragement and empty promises to "try harder" to serve their families. This will lead to more awkward interviews, and it will be more difficult to motivate yourself to continue meeting with them if it feels more and more awkward. This is why it is crucial that you establish consistent habits and structure to your interviews, so they are rejuvenating for them and leave more excitement to minister.

By the end of this chapter I hope that you will be able to: (1) prepare adequately for each interview, (2) know how to effectively begin the interview, (3) know what type of questions to ask during the interview, and (4) how to help ministering sisters and brothers leave the interview inspired.

Learn Their Name

I'll never forget Professor Butterfield who taught my accounting class when I was in business school at the University of Utah. She was always upbeat and passionate about teaching a subject she loved (I've never understood how someone could be passionate about accounting). There were about 100 students in an accounting class that was required for every business student. Something that comes as no surprise to my mother, accounting (or school in general) was never my strong suit. I began to struggle and get lost in that class. After a few weeks, I knew I needed to ask Professor Butterfield for help so I could figure out a plan or I wasn't going to pass the class. In these enormous college classes, the professor seemed so distant. When I approached professors of other courses, they would look at me like they had never seen me before when I had been in their class for weeks. But in this instance, it was surprisingly different. At the end of one particular class period, I slowly approached the front of the class as students filed out of the classroom and Professor Butterfield was erasing the day's lecture on the board. As I was ready to introduce myself and express my concern about my class performance she looked me in the eye with a look of familiarity and said, "Hey Kurt, what can I help you with?"

I was shocked! She knew my name, which made me feel like she knew me! I am not sure how she did this—whether she had been studying stacks of flashcards in her office late into the night or if she had a superpower. However she did it the fact that she knew my name established immediate trust with her that helped me feel comfortable expressing my concerns about the class. I knew if she cared enough to learn my name she cared enough to help me resolve my anxieties.

The first step in any leadership effort to influence individuals to follow you is to learn their names. I know… I know… you aren't good with names, right? Hogwash! That's just an excuse you tell yourself and others that means you haven't taken the time to learn a system of effectively learning names. There are a variety of resources you can find on LeadingSaints.org, and you can even spend some time in your Member Tools app studying pictures of members of your organization until you retain their names (hopefully they have taken the time to include a picture on ChurchofJesusChrist.org). However you want to do it, get it done! Obsess over it because the first step of sincerely knowing someone is knowing their name.

Prepare Their Minds

Have you ever been involved in a local mission or stake visit with Elder David A. Bednar of the Quorum of the Twelve? His approach in preparing the minds of those he is about to teach is incredible, and we could learn a lot from it. When Elder Bednar visits a mission or stake the president of that group will generally receive an email from Elder Bednar's secretary with a list of scriptures and/or conference talks that he requests every person read to be spiritually prepared for a "revelatory experience" rather than a meeting. Leaders need to take this same approach to turn these ministering interviews into ministering revelatory experiences. It doesn't have to be the same lengthy preparation one might go through before attending a three-hour meeting with Elder Bednar, but preparation is still needed. This preparation might be a scripture passage you ask them to read and ponder over before your interview, with a few questions they should expect you will ask. It does not need to be complicated or a huge task to complete before the interview, and as you do this, you will be able to accomplish a lot more than a dry start to the interview.

President David Fray in Houston, Texas, USA has a practical approach in helping prepare the minds of those he meets before a ministering interview. He has put together a Ministering Self-Evaluation form that he asks members of his elders quorum to fill out before the interview. There is a sample of the self-evaluation form in this chapter. In general, there is no right or wrong answer to these questions. The point is not to get everyone in the quorum to a place where they respond to each one with the ideal answer. This exercise is intended to find areas in which to best serve the assigned ministering families and to create further discussion during the ministering interview that will invite a revelatory experience.

Giving individuals a chance to fill out this evaluation form shifts the responsibility of evaluation from the Relief Society or elders quorum president to the individuals themselves. The questions on President Fray's form are what he and his presidency have developed. You could easily adjust this form so that it fits your purposes.

A CULTURE OF MINISTERING

THE MINISTER SELF-EVALUATION

PRIESTHOOD WORTHINESS

- I honestly strive to live the gospel to the best of my ability.
- I study the scriptures and pray daily.
- I actively seek opportunities to invite someone to do something that will bring them closer to Jesus Christ.
- I attend and participate in all my church meetings.
- I keep the Sabbath Day holy by participating in activities that will bring me closer to Christ.
- I fast once a month with a specific purpose.
- I am a full tithe payer. I pay tithing and a generous fast offering at least once a month.
- I am worthy to hold a current temple recommend.
- I seek to identify my ancestors who are waiting to receive the ordinances of the temple.
- I go to the temple frequently to perform temple ordinances for my ancestors.

PRIESTHOOD IN THE HOME

- I initiate family scripture study every day.
- I initiate family prayer every day.
- I initiate prayer with my wife every day.
- I initiate gospel study with my wife every day.
- I initiate Family Home Evenings in our home every week.
- I initiate frequent temple attendance with my wife.
- I initiate the giving of blessings to my family members.
- I honor my wife and strive to put her needs before my own.
- I speak softly to my wife with respect and kindness.
- I love and teach my children the gospel by example and words.
- I spend time with my children individually.

PRIESTHOOD IN THE MINISTRY

"Ministering is Christlike caring for others and helping meet their spiritual and temporal needs" (the First Presidency)

- I determine through inspiration and talking with the families the frequency and type of contact to have with them.
- I frequently visit with my assigned families and leave a tailored, spiritual message with them.
- I strive to take my companion with me on all ministry visits.
- I pray with my companion on how to help our families.
- I earnestly pray to the Lord by name for the members of the families assigned to me.
- I always respect the sacred calling of the father (or other head of household) by working through them, regardless of their church membership.
- I seek ways to gain the trust of and increase my friendship with my families.
- I actively look for opportunities to provide service to my families.
- I use every form of communication to respond to prompting of the Spirit to meet the needs of those I serve.
- I look for opportunities to befriend my families outside of regular ministry visits.
- I think of ways to help the fathers remain worthy and magnify their priesthood.
- I seek to help the individuals and families prepare for their next ordinances.
- I earnestly try to carry out the wishes of my priesthood leaders to help my ministry families.
- I immediately report any issues of concern to priesthood leaders that quorum or ward leadership should know about concerning the temporal and spiritual welfare of my families.
- I meet with my Priesthood leaders at least quarterly to render an account regarding my service and the needs and strengths of the families.

The Interview

As I have had the opportunity over the years to mentor various auxiliary leaders who know they should be doing stewardship interviews, the number one concern they have is that they don't know how to conduct a *one by one* interview. Many have attempted these interviews, and, after a few awkward encounters, they find anything else to do with their time as long as it doesn't include sitting in a room with someone else and asking them personal questions about their spiritual journey.

Though there is no perfect way to approach this interview and everyone will discover their style as they begin to conduct these interviews, allow me to give you a basic outline that can help you get started and then you can adjust it however you see fit. The outline includes three primary ways the Relief Society or quorum president should connect during the interview:

Connect Spiritually
Connect Personally
Connect Purposefully

Connect Spiritually

A crucial responsibility for a Relief Society or quorum leader is to set the tone for these interviews. They are short and straightforward, but they must still include the Spirit, or else they will feel like nothing more than an administrative checkbox you are only doing because you have to report it. Setting the tone spiritually can happen in a matter of minutes and usually includes starting with a prayer and sharing a spiritual thought.

DeAnna Murphy, a former stake Relief Society president in Minnesota, USA dedicated her focus as a stake Relief Society president to meeting with each ward Relief Society president on a regular basis. These ward Relief Society presidents didn't report to Sister Murphy, but she was there as a mentor and strived to connect to help each president develop and progress personally in her calling. In an interview on the Leading Saints podcast with Sister Murphy (which should be required listening), she mentioned how she would always ask the sister she was interviewing to say the opening prayer before the interview. This helped the president spiritually prepare for the discussion they were about to have.

Now that the prayer has been said setting a spiritual tone is necessary for the interview to continue to build a deeper connection as you go. Often I would share a short scripture and give my perspective on the verse and sometimes ask for their thoughts and reflection. What is important during this first step of connecting spiritually is to put yourself in a vulnerable position so that they in turn will feel more comfortable putting themselves in a vulnerable position. By sharing a scripture, and I mean sharing a scripture accompanied by tokens of your testimony, it shows them they are in a safe, non-judgmental place and will be more willing to open up and return the vulnerability. I'm not suggesting you share a scripture and weep as you share your testimony filled with clichés; instead, share the scripture and explain the spiritual journey you have gone through in the gospel. You might mention a trial from your past and how this scripture relates, or you could mention a universal human struggle that often surfaces in your life and how a particular scripture has brought you strength and hope. Again, I'm not suggesting you confess your deepest sins to this individual, but you are connecting spiritually by putting yourself in a vulnerable position and inviting them to do the same. Vulnerability is where a strong connection forms.

This exercise also puts the Relief Society or quorum president on the same level as the individual they are interviewing. As taught by DeAnna Murphy we never want them to feel like they are at the judgment bar ready to confess all their shortcomings of why they aren't better ministering sisters or brothers. Though you are the leader you don't want them to feel "presided over" during the interview, you want them to feel ministered to and that you are both children of God inviting the Spirit to teach both of you at that moment.

Connect Personally

As you consistently meet with each person or companionship on a quarterly basis, you will find the focus of each interview will vary between the three areas. There is nothing wrong with an interview that focuses on connecting spiritually. The next interview might be filled with conversation that connects personally. At the time of this writing, I was recently called as elders quorum president in a ward where I am not familiar with every elder (I moved in nine months before my call as elders quorum president). As I have been conducting ministering interviews, I have focused 90% of the interview on connecting personally. I want to hear a brother's story, where he is from, where he met his spouse, how they ended up in the area. As I have been doing this, I have found myself sitting back and listening to some incredible stories. Some have recounted their years of inactivity and the spiritual experiences that have brought them back to the gospel. Others have detailed their failed marriages and how the atonement of Jesus Christ has renewed them. Many of them tell a simple story of mission service, marrying in the temple, or completing formal education. Now when I see them in quorum meeting, I feel a connection beginning to form, a friendship that will bless both of our lives as we unite to minister to the ward.

DeAnna Murphy found it essential to ask them directly, "How are you doing—REALLY?" You might still get a short "I'm fine" answer but by first connecting spiritually your attempt to connect personally will come much easier with the Spirit present. Or if you have had them go through a similar ministering self-evaluation like President Fray does you could ask them, "What did you learn personally after taking that evaluation?"

    Taking the time to connect personally is vital on many levels, but most importantly it is building trust which will lead to commitment which leads to healthy group culture. When you build trust as a leader, others are willing to discuss anything with you. In May 2012, an article in The Atlantic reported that "in 1985, only 10 percent of Americans said they had no one with whom to discuss important matters, and 15 percent said they had only one such good friend. By 2004, 25 percent had nobody to talk to, and 20 percent had only one confidant." (https://theatln.tc/2IT5Jam). Our social media culture is disconnecting people personally faster than it is connecting people socially. I am sure in 2018 the percentage of people who feel like they have nobody with whom they can discuss important matters has only increased. When a local church leader takes the time to connect personally, you are giving them something they can't find in too many other venues, and it is something most are probably craving. If you get this step right, they will, in turn, get ministering right.

    As you notice the individual willing to be more vulnerable with you and more willing to personally connect it would be beneficial to have a set of questions that would invite them to expound on their spiritual journey. DeAnna Murphy often asks "what are you learning from the Spirit during your scripture study and personal time with the Savior?" Or you might consider some of the questions from President Fray's self-evaluation. Whatever questions you ask they should be introspective with no right or wrong answer. DeAnna Murphy talks about sweet moments when, after establishing spiritual and personal connections, the Relief Society president she was meeting with feel comfortable enough to share with her that she hadn't regularly been praying or hadn't been reading in the scriptures as often as she should or was struggling in her marriage. The sister felt she was in a no-judgment zone and had no hesitancy sharing such vulnerable information.

As I have mentioned before, there will be a handful of individuals in every Relief Society or quorum who are tough nuts to crack. No matter how hard you try or how vulnerable you get they will give you nothing more than one-word answers and do whatever it takes to get out of there. I smile when I think of a few individuals who were in my group back when I served as their high priest group leader. Some of those appointments were less than 2 minutes because I couldn't get them to expound on anything and I felt so awkward I rushed through it, got their report, and concluded the interview. These short interviews diminished as I developed my interviewing skills as a bishop. Don't be discouraged if some of the interviews remain awkward no matter how hard you try.

Connect Purposefully

Our general authority leaders taught that the purpose of ministering interviews is to counsel together about the wellbeing of the assigned ministering households. Because of this direction, many leaders will interpret the role of the ministering interview to be a simple interaction where you sit down with an individual or companionship, have a short prayer, and lead off with the questions, "How are your assigned families doing?" By this point, you can see the importance of first considering how you have connected spiritually and personally before you can effectively connect purposefully. If you jump in and lead off with a simple request for a report on the wellbeing of the families, you will most likely get a simple response such as, "Everything seems to be going fine" or a short and enthusiastic, "Good!" This then turns into a brief interview where not much information is exchanged because the Spirit was never established. Some may think I am overcomplicating this process, but the purpose of the interview isn't to find out that a father in the ward has lost a job or a mother in the ward has been in the hospital so that we can descend on their home with an army carrying casseroles. Of course, if there is a major concern like unemployment or failing health that information should have already been communicated the same day the ministering sister or brother learned of it. The deeper purpose of the ministering interview is helping the ministering sister or brother take steps that will build a strong relationship and connection to each family rather than just sending them in as spies to report on anything out of the ordinary. The relationship and connection are what will build a culture of ministering within the ward. Most people don't want to share with ward members their deepest trials until they have found safety in a relationship that has been fostered by a consistent personal connection. "How are your families doing?" shouldn't be your first question, it should be one of your last.

A poignant way of connecting with an individual and also helping them find purpose in their assignment is by the leader asking specific open-ended questions. In another interview on the Leading Saints podcast with DeAnna Murphy, she discussed in more detail the four questions she would ask in her *one by one* interviews when she was a stake Relief Society president:

How are you—REALLY? (Connecting Personally)

What are you learning from the Spirit in your scripture study and your personal time with the Savior? (Connecting Spiritually & Personally)

What are you learning in your ministering assignment? (Connecting Spiritually & Purposefully)

Tell me about the families you are serving and what do I need to be aware of in terms of their needs and strengths? (Connecting Purposefully)

This simple format of asking these four questions can have a huge impact on the individuals a leader interviews. They invite each individual to be introspective and ponder over each answer before they share it. It builds the connection you need with each individual so that they not only want to follow you as their leader but they also want to serve those to whom they are assigned.

It doesn't have to be four questions. It might be seven questions or ten questions. Whatever you come up with as a leader is fine. Test different questions and you will discover those that make the most sense for you.

As you ask ministering sisters and brothers about the families they are assigned to, this is also a perfect opportunity to ask about families that live near them. Remember the power of propinquity? As an elders quorum president, I have made it clear that each ministering brother is not just responsible for their "assigned families" but also the families that live near them. I have set the expectation that I will be asking about those families as well during our ministering interviews even if that family is assigned to a different companionship.

Finally, ministering interviews create an excellent opportunity to reference the Relief Society or quorum vision statement (*Title of Liberty*) and see if they find personal purpose and motivation in the statement. If they do, great, you can leverage that and apply it to their ministering efforts. If they don't find personal purpose or motivation, you can talk that through and figure out how you could customize it to their situation so that they do see a role they can play in bringing the vision statement into reality.

All This in 15 Minutes?

As we approach the end of this chapter, you are

probably thinking, "You are expecting me to accomplish all these steps within a 15-minute interview?" It is quite overwhelming but take it interview by interview. As a new Relief Society or quorum leader, it might take two to three short interviews with each individual to establish rapport, or as we said in the mission field, build a relationship of trust. After two to three interviews, you will find some momentum created by the connection you have established. Once individuals feel like they are sitting down with a leader who understands and knows them the interview process accelerates. The points established in this chapter shouldn't be seen as a checklist. Some ministering interviews will focus on building a personal connection and others will focus on building a purposeful connection. Don't put pressure on yourself—enjoy the process of getting to know those you lead on a deeper level and build a friendship.

Onboarding

As is the nature of a Latter-day Saint ward, from time to time you will get a new person moving into your ward or someone who is newly baptized. It's important to meet with these members as soon as possible and help them understand the Relief Society or quorum culture to integrate themselves into the mission of the group. Whitney Johnson, in her book *Building an A-Team*, says there are three steps to onboarding a new employee (or in this case a new Relief Society or quorum member). First, figure out the best way to communicate the group's vision. Second, do your best to understand their personal "why" and what they are looking for in a Relief Society or quorum experience. Third, give them a personal vision that will help you gauge how they are integrating into the culture of the group. With so much tradition in Latter-day Saint culture, you might have some people struggle with the cultural structure you have established in your Relief

Society or quorum, and some might not respond to it as well as others. Consistent, regular, short interviews, in the beginning, will make sure they are not lost in the momentum.

In short, don't assume everyone who joins your Relief Society or quorum will naturally catch the cultural wave. Without building the full context of the experience, they could be overwhelmed by the unfamiliar energy and disengage.

Ministering Interviews Are First Downs, Not Touchdowns

Imagine a football game with no scoreboard. Also, imagine you don't know how many yards away the end zone is. The field could be 100 yards or 1100 yards, maybe only 25 yards. If you were the football coach in this type of league what would your game plan be? The best coaches would urge you to focus on getting first downs since you have no clue how far down the field the goal is. As long as you keep getting first downs within four plays, you would at some point start scoring points.

Consider it's third down and your offense has eight yards to go to reach the first down marker. The quarterback drops back in the pocket waiting for his receivers to get open. All his receivers are covered so he scrambles. He gets slowed down by a linebacker but gains enough yardage to put the ball across the first-down line. The team goes crazy with celebration! They rush the field and put the quarterback on their shoulders and carry him off the field to the locker room. But it was only a first down. Why would you celebrate a first down when a touchdown is the goal?

Now that the reporting metric for leaders is quarterly ministering interviews it is going to be easy to make these interviews the focus of all that you do as a leader. While not a bad idea, what happens over time is that you lose sight of the primary goal (the end zone) which is creating a culture of ministering so that each family in your ward feels supported and part of a larger ward culture of love. Leaders can easily reach for 100% ministering interviews and puff out their chest as they submit their report assuming they are an incredible leader who is winning the Superbowl of church leadership! Don't get caught celebrating first downs instead of touchdowns.

The Lord has defined the purpose of ministering (or the game): to "watch over... and be with and strengthen them" (D&C 20:53). ...to "warn, expound, exhort, and teach, and invite all to come unto Christ" (D&C 20:59). Our coaches (15 prophets, seers, and revelators) realize it's not the same length of the field for each assigned ministering sister or brother. For Sister Widow it might be a long way down until she feels at peace with the passing of her husband. For the Washburn family, it's a short field because they need new friends in the ward into which they recently moved. Ministering doesn't have a clear focus or goal line. We want to fellowship families and make sure they have a member support group around them, but we rarely know when we have scored points or won the game. The coaches (15 prophets, seers, and revelators) realize they can't point to a scoreboard and there is no standard field length they can measure. So, what are we supposed to tell their local leaders? They have to find a focus—something they can measure and track. So, they ask us to at least get the first down (interview members of your Relief Society or quorum at least quarterly) and then keep pushing for the next first down. The more consistent the ministering interviews are, the more likely members of your group will take action to connect with their assigned families until scoring a "touchdown."

Some "touchdowns" are easier than others, but they should all be defined before the team runs out on the field. It is up to the ministering sisters or brothers (with help from their leaders) to pray about the family, discuss it as a companionship, and then decide on the primary goal for the assigned family. Do they need to be sealed as a family? Do they need to become active in church attendance? Do they only need a strong spiritual message in their home that is coming from someone other than the parents? Whatever the goal is make sure it is well-defined. Ultimately, our coaches have identified helping each member receive the next saving ordinance they need as a touchdown.

So, the next time you want to celebrate your ministering interview consistency—remember, though the Philadelphia Eagles won the Superbowl they were ranked number four in making first downs. The ministering interview is a marker, not the goal.

Bring an Extra Chair

This goal of this chapter is not to give you the perfect system of conducting a ministering interview. Preferably, I hope that it will activate the leadership center of your brain so that you can begin to approach your ministering interviews with a clear purpose that leads to establishing a culture of ministering in your Relief Society or quorum.

I've made many references to the interviews I have done with DeAnna Murphy. She is indeed a leader of our time blessed with a unique ability to tap into and articulate the principles of servant leadership. I love her general approach to these ministering interviews—feeling humble and unqualified as the leader. She talks about first being called as a stake Relief Society president and setting a goal to meet with each ward Relief Society president on a monthly basis. She would begin each interview with three chairs, leaving one empty as a symbol that the Savior was there with them. "…where two or three are gathered together in my name… there will I be in the midst of them…" (D&C 6:32) She would often remark to those women that she wasn't entirely sure what she was doing or what was supposed to be accomplished during that interview. But she would bring an extra chair to the interview to help her and the sister she was meeting with remember that Christ was their leader and together they might discover the topics and focus He would have them discuss.

As you conduct these crucial ministering interviews, don't burden yourself with unneeded pressure. You are merely an imperfect vessel given the charge to connect with those you lead, not merely to check off an arbitrary box each quarter, but instead, to develop a deep connection with each member of your Relief Society or quorum. If they know their leader knows and loves them, they will begin to lead themselves and contribute to the overall culture of ministering that will start to bring people unto Jesus Christ, our leader. The greatest ministering in a ward will not happen in the homes of assigned families, it will happen in the ministering interview between an individual and their leader.

KURT FRANCOM

CHAPTER 4: LED BY THE SPIRIT

"*Verily I say, men should be anxiously engaged in a good cause, and do many things of their own free will, and bring to pass much righteousness;*" - Doctrine & Covenants 58:27

The announcement of the retirement of home and visiting teaching and the new implementation of ministering led to several weeks where Relief Societies and quorums discussed these topics. During these discussions it was not uncommon to hear phrases like:

"We can finally do what we should have been doing all along and just serve our families!"

"I'm so glad we don't have to 'check the box' to feel like we have done a good job."

"It's like we are living a higher law."

I would generally agree with many of these statements, and at the time of the announcement, it was exciting to have this new ministering program that infused new energy into our Relief Society and quorum meetings. However, we all experienced some level of ex-girlfriend syndrome where the old program isn't just the prior program, but it was an inferior program.

As Relief Society and quorum presidents attempted to implement the ministering program, it appears they were trying too hard not to make it look much like home or visiting teaching. Instead of removing just the monthly reporting facet of home teaching we unintentionally removed all the habits of home teaching, including the monthly visit. Though monthly visits aren't "required" in ministering it doesn't mean it wasn't an effective way to minister. Sure, back when we did visiting and home teaching it often felt rote and insincere. It wasn't that people meant for it to be that way, even back then they wanted to "minister," they didn't know how. So, they would say, "I want to be a good home teacher but I don't know what else to do, so I will at least visit my families once a month." Now, without the structure of home teaching, they might say, "I want to be a good ministering brother, but I don't know what to do, so I will at least… um… let's see… I will at least… I don't know what to do."

I'll be the first to agree that home teaching got a bit stale after 50+ years, but we must recognize the structure it offered to those wanting to serve. A monthly visit might not have been the most effective approach for many families, but it did get many visiting and home teachers out of their house and interacting with their assigned families.

The direction in April 2018 included the importance of being led by Spirit in one's ministering efforts.

> ***"How is ministering led by the Spirit?"*** *As members minister, they seek inspiration to know how best to reach out to others and meet their needs. Would a scheduled visit and regular phone calls to an older sister who lives alone provide the connection she needs? Would an invitation to a less-active young adult to participate in a community project be the most helpful*

contact? Would supporting a youth's soccer game help both the youth and her parents? Would texting someone a hope-filled scripture help lighten his burdens? Would a note or card or email show helpful concern? What would the Savior have His servants do? Finding inspired answers to such questions and using all available methods for making contact with those they are assigned is central to inspired ministering. To provide Christ-like service, ministering sisters and brothers cannot rely on routine visits or predetermined messages; they seek inspiration and counsel with family members to best care for those to whom they are assigned—using the time and resources they have." (Ministering Frequently Asked Questions) https://www.churchofjesuschrist.org/ministering/ministering-faq?lang=eng

The Spirit leads inspired ministering, and that process can be much more difficult than a monthly visit. You may face the hurdle of this shift in emphasis when ministering sisters and brothers dismiss the monthly visit, and that was a structure that helped them do something before. You might have noticed as a leader that even those who never missed a month in the visiting and home teaching effort are now rarely doing anything. It is easy to assume this is a motivation problem when in reality it is an ability problem. Visiting or home teachers completed the "check the box" action item of the monthly visit—now they are expected to think of unique and personalized ways to serve, and that doesn't come naturally. It will be up to the Relief Society or quorum leadership to create structure and action items so that ministering sisters and brothers can rely on the nature of habit and routine to effectively build relationships with their assigned families.

Establishing Structure

Visiting and home teachers have shared remarkable experiences of having dramatic spiritual promptings leading them to randomly show up at a home or making a phone call right when the family most needed help. These are faith-promoting experiences, but we cannot expect them to be routine. When we are encouraged to follow the Spirit that doesn't mean ministering sisters and brothers should pray at home until a random prompting pops into their head. As President Nelson said, "…I know that good inspiration is based upon good information."

As a leader, your role is to help individuals in your Relief Society or quorum receive spiritual guidance so that they can effectively serve assigned families. The best way to start doing this is to help everyone establish a touchpoint or trigger with each family, much like we had built in with the visiting and home teaching programs. There are several ways of doing this, but a powerful way to create structure is to visit an assigned family on a regular basis and counseling together as a companionship (or with the Relief Society or quorum president) and establish the touchpoint or trigger that will create a routine in your service. One starting point could be to ask families what specific ministering efforts they would like or need.

For example, a good brother in my elders quorum who had decades of home teaching consistency before the retirement of that program took it upon himself to visit each assigned ministering family with his youth companion and ask each household how they could best serve them as ministering brethren. One household consisted of two single sisters who shared that they enjoy and benefit from a monthly visit and a lesson. Another household included a former bishop of the ward who is a service missionary in another ward. He wanted to receive a consistent phone call to be made aware of happenings in the ward, such as mission calls, ward activities, etc. He also requested a regular visit that didn't necessarily have to be monthly.

Meeting each family in their home and asking what they need from ministering visits creates a structure that appeals to our human nature. It allows us to have a similar experience as the visiting and home teaching experience because now you have specific prompts that keep you engaged with the family. The fact that visiting and home teaching felt like a "check the box" program wasn't a bad thing; it was likely less effective because everyone's box to check looked the same. We still need boxes to check to keep us engaged, and hopefully, we can customize those boxes to be just what the family needs.

Feeding the Fire

Anyone who has been at Scout camp out knows there are always one or two boys who take on the responsibility to keep the fire going. They probably love fire so much that they are the ones who start the fire on each campout. As each log burns down, the Scouts proactively add logs, so the fire keeps burning brightly for all to enjoy.

Each Relief Society and quorum president should take on a similar role in their organization. You can't make everyone feel a spiritual prompting related to their families, but you can keep the fire and excitement of the ministering program going so that they are consistently open to spiritual direction. Fanning the flame includes consistent ministering interviews as discussed in previous chapters as well as throughout the Sunday experience at church.

During the days of the home teaching program, it was common for priesthood holders to hear about it each week during opening exercises. A bishopric member would give each quorum an opportunity to share announcements with the group, which usually led to the elders quorum president or high priest group leader to stand and say (almost verbatim), "Brethren, the end of the month is coming quickly, please get out and visit your home teaching families." I wouldn't have called this the most effective tactic, but it was part of our Latter-day Saint tradition.

Priesthood opening exercises is an opportunity for an

elders quorum president to interface with all members of his quorum, even those serving in the Young Men program. I am sure the Relief Society presidency could take a similar opportunity at the beginning of their meeting but may have to find a chance to address the sisters and youth in Young Women and Primary.

To give you an idea of what this might look like, a few weeks ago during priesthood opening exercises they asked me if I had anything from the elders quorum. I took a few minutes and invited each person to take out their smartphone and open Member Tools. I then guided the group to where they can find their ministering assignment and companion so that they never have to rely on a printed assignment again. I then encouraged each person to take the time that Sunday to learn the names of each person in their assigned families. It was similar to the prior process, but I was drawing their attention to their assignment and inviting them to be open to spiritual guidance.

101 Ways to Minister

Remember the remarkable story told in general conference by Elder Jeffrey R. Holland after the announcement of the new ministering effort? He told of a relationship between two good ward friends, Brett and Edwin. Edwin was Brett's home teacher, but that formality had turned into a strong friendship. When Brett's wife suddenly collapsed with a severe medical condition, the first phone call Brett made was to Edwin requesting his help in that very moment. Sadly, Brett's wife passed away, but the story speaks of a remarkable home teaching relationship that was so much more and in the moment of crisis Brett knew whom to call.

This type of relationship should not be expected merely because a Relief Society or elders quorum president decided to assign someone to some family. Consistent caring over time built a relationship of trust so that in the moment of crisis Brett was not obligated to call his "home teacher," rather he called his "friend" who happened to be his home teacher.

Stephen Covey, the author of many books including *7 Habits of Highly Effective People*, taught a powerful principle of emotional bank accounts. We all have emotional bank accounts with everyone in our life, especially those with whom we have formed a relationship. Little habits and interactions we do in life related to those around us either make an emotional deposit or an emotional withdrawal. When my wife gets home and sees that I have straightened up the house, that's an emotional deposit. When I am kind, patient, and sensitive to her needs, my emotional account balance continues to go up. From time to time I have to make an emotional withdrawal when specific deadlines are demanding my attention, and I have to lock myself in a room and work, and I can't help with the children and other home demands. When that withdrawal happens, I better have a positive account balance from past deposits, or else it is going to damage our relationship.

This same analogy applies to the relationship created through the ministering effort. We often hear of a family facing a difficult time and our culture assumes they should reach out to their ministering sisters or brothers for help, but if those ministering sisters or brothers haven't made emotional deposits over time with the family there will be no reason for members to make that phone call.

Part of the role of Relief Society and elders quorum presidencies is to encourage these small efforts of emotional deposits so that in the moment of highest need families will have someone to call.

One way to help build emotional deposits is to be proactive in bringing ideas to those you lead on how they can do this week to week. I need to mention again the good resources President David Fray from Houston, TX, USA has been putting together (he hates the fact that I keep mentioning his name in this book, but he deserves the credit). He recently sent me a list he was putting together of ways ministering sisters or brothers could minister to their assigned families. There weren't quite 101 ways on his list, but I hope we can get there as more of the Leading Saints audience sends us ideas.

I love this list because I have been using it during priesthood opening exercises to foster some ideas of how the members of my quorum could be proactive in ministering to their assigned families. I stand up during my given time and say, "Brethren, a great way to minister to your assigned families is to wish them well on their birthday or any other family anniversary. Consider taking time today to find out who on your assigned list has a birthday next and prepare accordingly."

For reference here are 101 ways to minister (at least we are getting closer to 101 ways):

1. Invite them over for dinner
2. Share a family home evening
3. Offer to babysit
4. Invite them to lunch
5. Celebrate their successes
6. Send them conference talks
7. Help with rides for their kids
8. Do little service projects for them
9. Send them an encouraging message
10. Sit next to them at church
11. Ask them for advice
12. Drop off a treat with a note
13. Remember their birthday/anniversaries
14. Attend kids school events
15. Call them to talk and listen
16. Memorize each person's name
17. Invite them to a game night
18. Do a double date with the parents
19. Go to the temple with them

20. Find a way to help them with their calling
21. Invite them to attend ward choir practice
22. Offer to pick up their mail while they are on vacation
23. Help them minister to their assigned ministering families
24. Offer a priesthood blessing
25. Put their names on the temple prayer roll
26. Shovel their walks after a snowstorm
27. Help with a home project
28. Offer a ride to a ward activity
29. Have a block party so you can invite them to it
30. Take them to lunch
31. Feed the missionaries together
32. Text a scripture or quote to them
33. Communicate the ward announcements to them when they miss church
34. Deliver a spiritual message in their home
35. Teach a skill or talent to their children
36. Show them how to use a helpful smartphone app
37. Comment on a social media post they shared
38. Help with their family history or ask for their help with yours
39. Help them upload their picture to Member Tools
40. Show them how to use the Gospel Library app
41. Find out which of their family members lives closest to them and how those family members help them
42. Cook extra of a meal and drop off a plate of food
43. Sign up for a service assignment together
44. On Facebook, turn on notifications for their account or mark them as "See First"
45. Show them how to use social media to share their testimony and to be a digital missionary online
46. Visit them once a month and share a spiritual thought (yes, this is still legal)
47. Plan a vacation with both of your families

48. Teach them how to log into their ChurchofJesusChrist.org account
49. Help them upload a picture to their ChurchofJesusChrist.org account
50. Review all the church apps with them and show them how to use them to enhance their gospel experience
51. Do indexing with them
52. When they go on vacation offer to watch pets or water their plants
53. Connect with their ministering sister/brothers and work together to serve them
54. Get general conference tickets and attend together
55. Take a treat to the family on general conference weekend
56. Invite them to attend the priesthood/women's meeting together at your local stake center
57. Deliver a summary of the most recent conference talks with written notes about your favorite messages.
58. Help them download and become familiar with all the Latter-day Saint related smartphone apps
59. Help them update their personal information on the Member Tools app
60. Help them learn how to discover uplifting Latter-day Saint content online including social media, YouTube, and podcasts
61. Help them visit all the neighbors around their home (Latter-day Saints and non-members) and ask them if they would be willing to serve others in the area when a need arises. Gather their names and phone numbers which will establish a friendly relationship.

Many Don't Need Ministering Brothers or Sisters

We often hear what I call "back-of-the-Ensign-stories" that are incredibly faith-building and demonstrate the tender mercies of the Lord (much like Elder Holland's conference story about Edwin and Brett). After reading these inspiring stories, we forget that they are often the exception rather than the rule. Just because a ministering sister or brother can suddenly turn into a hero for a particular family doesn't mean this will always be the case. Sometimes, families don't need ministering sisters or brothers to that degree.

Let me give you an example. A few years ago, my mom attended a routine medical checkup, and the doctors discovered a condition that had the potential of being life-threatening. Thankfully, it was found early enough that a simple outpatient surgery resolved the issue and she is happy and healthy to this day. In preparing for and after her surgery she needed some help. For about a week she was in no condition to do simple house chores or cook dinner (and if you know my dad, he has no business cooking). My mom had great home and visiting teachers who consistently visited her and whom she considered to be friends, but she didn't call them during this time. Why? Was she being too prideful and not willing to accept anyone's service? No. The reality is she has four children who live relatively close to her. Each of those children has a competent spouse, and together we all chipped in as a family and helped out. As her children, we all took a turn bringing in meals, doing house chores, and making sure we covered most responsibilities so that my mom could recover from her surgery and then get back to the routines of her life. It worked out great!

Many times, as we talk about the ministering program, we interpret it as an effort to interject ourselves into the lives of those we are assigned to so that in the moment of trial we can all drown them in casseroles and questions of, "Is there anything we can do for you?" The reality is many people already have a support infrastructure in place and when the moment of crisis hits, they have a list of people (typically close family) they can call long before they ever consider calling their ministering sisters or brothers.

As a leader, you might find individuals frustrated that the families they are assigned never let them serve. When families have a challenge where the ministering sisters or brothers could help, the family doesn't call, and we see it as a missed opportunity. But we must realize that even though we are a church with a ministering program, we are also a church that promotes self-reliance. We don't stop our habit of acquiring food storage so that when hard times hit we have to rely on our ministering brothers or sisters to bring us food; instead, we are encouraged to gather food storage so that we are less dependent on others. The same principle applies to ministering; if we have family or other support in our life, we may find no reason to rely on ministering sisters or brothers. As a leader, you may have to continue to encourage the ministering sisters or brothers who serve an assigned family that is more self-reliant than others. In this case, remember the importance of organizing assigned families by need so that those without an extensive support system are high on the list and have great ministering brothers and sisters assigned to them.

It will also be easy for ministering sisters or brothers of self-reliant families to diminish their influence in this family's life because they "don't feel needed." Through the encouragement of their leader, they can find more fundamental ways to minister that will still bless the family. We don't have to steady the waters of a crisis to minister; it might be as easy as a monthly visit where you share your testimony.

Introverts

A few years ago, I came across a book by Susan Cain

titled *Quiet: The Power of Introverts in a World That Can't Stop Talking*. I always thought I understood what an introvert was (an individual who is quiet, socially awkward, and avoids all situations of interaction) and I never considered myself to be an introvert. However, halfway through the book I suddenly realized I had many introvert tendencies than I originally thought. I had assumed that because I am a personable, outgoing individual, I must be an extrovert. In reality, I prefer staying home, staying out of the big crowds, and relaxing in the quiet of familiar spaces. Not only was I shocked that I had many characteristics of an introvert, by the end of the book I was proud of being one!

Here's a glimpse of a new perspective I gained regarding Latter-day Saint introverts. The author explains that the difference between extroverts and introverts depends on how they react to different stimuli. Extroverts require lots of stimuli to function at their best. Introverts need minimal stimuli to perform at their best. Extroverts love being out socializing on a Friday night while introverts enjoy staying home and reading a book. If introverts go to the party, they are over-stimulated and outside their comfort level. They might not run out of the party screaming, but they wouldn't be overly comfortable and seek a quiet spot away from others. If extroverts stayed at home reading a book, they may experience cabin fever and be restless. These two examples are not an attempt to determine if you are an extrovert or an introvert. Everyone has a mixture of each. Nobody is 100% either way.

Are We a Church for Extroverts?

Since reading the book *Quiet* and gaining a deeper understanding of introverts I have often found myself identifying "good" fellowshipping ideas. Except that they are probably good for extroverts, but terrifying for introverts. For example, it is typical in a ward council to bring up a name of a family or individual who has withdrawn from the ward. The council might discuss the family's life situations and share concerns about them, and then the typical idea to resolve the problem, "Let's go visit them!" Or, if the whole ward could be more unified, it is often suggested to have a social gathering to foster discussion and relationship. These might seem like great ideas, but from an introvert's point of view, they are terrible ideas.

As leaders encourage ministering sisters and brothers to seek spiritual promptings, they should recognize many efforts in the church culture favors extroverts:

- We organize activities to foster social connections
- We spend two of the three hours at the church where discussion and interaction are encouraged
- We are asked periodically to stand in front of more than 100 people and speak in sacrament meeting
- We are asked to share our beliefs with family and friends who are not members
- We applaud members who are go-getters and socially outgoing

Are We a Church for Introverts?

Even though the Latter-day Saint experience (or any Christian experience) caters to extroverts, we do have unique aspects in our church and culture that are designed well for introverts:

- We attend a weekly sacrament meeting where we take several minutes to sit in silence and ponder the sacrifice of our Savior
- We show respect for God with reverence and

solitude which includes avoiding loud applause during our services
- We savor time in the celestial room in our temples for quiet pondering and reflection
- We study from the scriptures individually and pray in secret daily

If someone is assigned a family or an individual whose personality is more introverted should we be approaching them differently than calling and demanding a time to come and visit in their home? Could the fact that someone wants to enter into their home—their "happy place," their sanctuary—be so outside their comfort zone that they dread the experience? Maybe the introvert who is strongly encouraged to attend the ward party is so uncomfortable that the act of "fellowshipping" is just the thing that contributes to inactivity.

Consider the story that someone told in the form of a comment on LeadingSaints.org. She speaks of her father who was very ill and discouraged by persistent home teachers. "My father was a very private man. He was very ill and mostly bedridden for the last two years of his life—but some of his closest friends were not even aware of that fact because he was so private. Home teachers became increasingly frustrated that my mother would not schedule appointments when they called, so one time they refused to talk to her, and my dad had to get out of bed to answer the call. He told them it was not convenient to see them. At some point, they showed up unannounced, and my mom [would not let them in.]"

Not only is it draining for introverts to socialize, if they are given a list of unfamiliar names and expected to call them or make routine visits, that might be asking more of that member than the leader might recognize. For extroverts, this task is no problem, introverts may feel they are standing on the edge of the high dive.

I received an email about this topic from a brother who

shared an experience from a ward council discussion. He relates the following: "We had ongoing discussions in our ward council about increasing our efforts to do missionary work. The council wanted to challenge members to have five non-member families in their homes each month. I tried to explain to them that it might be easy for some, but for many families, it is not. These families don't allow members in their homes, let alone non-members."

Relief Society and elders quorum presidents might pause the next time she or he is frustrated with someone not engaging in the ministering program. The difficulty of the task is relative to an individual's comfort level. My intention isn't to suggest we are doing things wrong or to give alternative solutions. This insight was a new perspective that caught me off guard. I had never considered that visits from members might be discouraging for some to engage in the Latter-Day Saint experience.

How to Minister to Introverts

I can be a very outgoing and gregarious person. Serving as a bishop and in other higher profile callings, I was generally the one working the room and being the social butterfly at most ward functions. However, I am an introvert. Even though I pushed myself to be Mr. Social as a leader, I would often come home completely drained of energy, wanting to block out the world and recharge by watching a movie or having a more in-depth interaction with my family. I say this because it is essential to realize that introverts are not always the ones sitting awkwardly in the corner all by themselves or avoiding social interactions altogether. It might be safe to assume someone is more introverted than extroverted. Regarding ministering, I often dread the experience of someone coming over to my house and prodding me to have a conversation about my life and "how things are going." However, I have had several home teachers in the past who have made an extra effort or who I have related to better who became friends. I then looked forward to having them in my home or sitting with them at a ward activity.

If a ministering sister or brother feels like a relationship with another is superficial and almost awkward, it may be safe to assume that person is an introvert. Here are a few approaches to consider to minister to an introvert effectively:

Aim for depth, not breadth — Social interactions can be very draining for introverts. If your primary interaction with them is at church and the conversations stay superficial ("How's your job?" "What did you do this weekend?" etc.), it is going to be a negative experience that the introvert wants to avoid. Introverts still enjoy conversation, but they prefer to do it with those they have a deeper connection with, those they consider a friend. A ministering sister or brother will need to make an extra effort to establish a friendship with them to earn the trust and friendship they seek. Once you've established a friendship, they will look forward to having you in their home and their life. To do this, aim for more profound interaction with them, instead of asking, "How's work?" consider questions like, "What led you to go into that field? Do you find your day-to-day job fulfilling?"

Check in less frequently — Again, social interactions are quite draining on an introvert. Instead of the monthly in-home visit consider every other month or once a quarter and then supplement the communication via text, social media, or written letter.

Be nearby — For an introvert, the church experience can go from pleasant to uncomfortable at the drop of a hat. They might be in a gospel doctrine class enjoying their reflection over a scripture passage when suddenly the teacher asks them to turn to their neighbor and interact with them. As a ministering sister or brother, it is essential for you to stay close during a church function ready to show them a friend is nearby. Sit next to them in Sunday School, but that doesn't mean you have to "small talk." At the moment social interaction is forced upon them they will be relieved to see they have already connected with the person sitting next to them. This same principle applies to ward activities as well. They would much rather sit by someone they have a connection with than sitting alone as an introvert.

Don't think about it too much — Introverts are not a strange human species, and I hesitate to write this section of the book because it is not like an introvert is going to scream and run from the room if you do the wrong things. Mainly it is helpful to understand generally how an introvert ticks so that you don't misunderstand them if they seem distant or almost trying to avoid you. It's better to assume they are more of an introvert than thinking they don't like you.

"They're Fine."

I laughed out loud when I came across this Facebook post:

For those of you not familiar, The Babylon Bee is a satirical Christian website that produces fake articles that help Christians laugh at their culture (in a fun way). This article tells of a Methodist pastor who took an informal survey of his congregation and was happy to hear that every single person was doing either "fine," "good," or "real good."

They quote this (fictional) pastor, "It's really quite spectacular," the pastor told reporters Monday. "You would think, given the state of our fallen world, that at least one person would be going through a crisis or battling some kind of indwelling sin that they need help with. But not at this church—we're all doing fine it seems.

Praise the Lord!"

They create irony in the satirical article by observing a woman from the congregation "was later spotted at a coffee shop, bawling her eyes out over some personal struggle, according to sources."

I laughed because I'm afraid that after a few months of ministering interviews the interviews might go like this:

Relief Society President: "How are your ministering families doing?"
Ministering Sister: "They're fine."
Relief Society President: "Great! Thanks for meeting with me."

The only way to avoid this is through leadership that fosters their spiritual interactions and keeps them intentional about how they are serving those they are assigned to. We must coach each companionship on the difficult path of creating deep connection and friendship. We must get past the "I'm doing fine."

Conclusion

President Russell T. Osguthorpe, former General Sunday School President, shared a remarkable story of persistently following the Spirit as a ministering brother or sister during his 2011 BYU Devotional address:

My wife's brother Steve became less active in the Church at the age of 15. He married outside the Church and for many years asked that home teachers not visit him. This is how Steve tells his own story:

"I was assigned a home teacher. When he called me, I said something like, "I don't want to be contacted, and my wife is not interested." He asked if he could at least make contact once in a while and made sure I understood he was there for us if a need arose."

"For 22 years, every month, I faithfully received a postcard from that home teacher with a kind thought or just a "hello, hope things are going well for you." I had never met him for the first 18 years, yet every month he made his home teaching contact the only way he could."

"That contact became very important to me when we found out my wife had brain cancer in 1996. We never had children, and so I was the primary caregiver for her during her 23-month illness. I was helped by twelve wonderful women who were friends, neighbors, or co-workers."

"One day the ward Relief Society president came by our home to offer help. My wife was asleep at the time, and I didn't want to wake her, so that visit never happened. But that contact by the Relief Society president was more important to me, I think, as it softened my heart. My wife of 31 years passed away ten days later."

Following his wife's death, Steve needed help in planning the funeral. Who do you think he turned to for that help? To his home teacher of 22 years—the one who had faithfully written all of those cards! How easy would it have been for that home teacher not to complete his calling? Some of us have a difficult time home teaching people who do welcome us. But he stayed with it.

Five years later, Steve remarried. His second wife was a faithful member of the Church. His pathway back to full activity in the Church began. Last year Steve was ordained a priest, and then he received the Melchizedek Priesthood—all after 50 years of inactivity in the Church.

When we care for someone, we want to do something for them. Steve's home teacher cared enough to do something—to write literally hundreds of cards to the one he'd been assigned to visit. The Relief Society president cared enough to visit at exactly the right moment for Steve. I am convinced that there are people all around us who need that kind of caring, that kind of love. All we need to do is open our eyes and our ears and our hearts so that we can know what we need to do for others." (*What If Love Were Our Only Motive? https://speeches.byu.edu/talks/*)

As we strive to create a culture of ministering in our Relief Society or quorum, I hope we can stoke the fires of inspiration through the Spirit. This is an excellent opportunity to lead others, not by telling them what to do, but by encouraging them to carve out moments when they can petition the heavens to inspire them to bless their families through simple actions of service that will build a relationship of trust and help them be a servant of the Lord at the moment they are needed most.

CHAPTER 5: MOTIVATING SAINTS

"When obedience ceases to be an irritant and becomes our quest, in that moment God will endow us with power."

- *Ezra Taft Benson*

A few years ago (during the days of the home teaching program), when I was serving as high priests group leader, I was asked to lead a training session at a stake leadership meeting that included all elders quorum presidents, high priests group leaders, and high councilors in my stake. I started by posing the following question, "What is the main reason people don't home teach?" Instantly, as if he knew I was going to ask this question, someone from the back of the room firmly stated, "LAZINESS!" The answer didn't surprise me as much as his quick response. Was he right? Is laziness the entire problem? Are we a church full of men who can't pull themselves away from Netflix or video games to minister to their neighbor?

When I was an elders quorum president in the young single adult ward, I started to think laziness was the problem as well. I thought it had to be! I put in hours every month organizing, printing, highlighting, distributing routes to each member of his quorum. If one of the elders wasn't there the last Sunday of the month to receive next month's home teaching assignment, I would mail it to him so he would get it by Tuesday. The elders of my quorum could never claim they didn't know their assignment. I felt I was on top of it. I tried to retain the details of each route. If the bishop asked me who home taught a specific person, I wanted to fire off the answer in 0.3 seconds. I was a motivated leader and wanted to see change happen. Then, at the end of the month, when things didn't change, I wondered what more could have been done? I felt like I had done my part. My conclusion was the same as many other leaders. It must be the home teachers. In frustration, we seek for a logical answer, and we hastily label our priesthood brothers as "lazy."

But are those men and women really lazy who fail to minister effectively? A closer understanding of their life may show a different side of the story. We are talking about men and women who are considered active in the Church. They get up each Sunday and get themselves and their families ready. Many of these individuals have full-time jobs or run a hectic household to do what is required to provide for their family. It is hard to assume that laziness has captured their heart when they are asked to minister.

Fundamental Attribution Error

I never intended to turn this book into a deep study of the psychology of the human psyche, but let's face it, the history of home/visiting teaching (and now ministering) is one of the longest-running case studies of human nature and influence. If one can understand how individuals respond to tasks like ministering, we can begin to find ideas that will overcome the barriers. We must start by understanding the *Fundamental Attribution Error*.

Fundamental Attribution Error *is our tendency to explain someone's behavior based on internal factors, such as personality or disposition, and to underestimate the influence that external factors, such as situational influences, have on another person's behavior.*
(https://study.com/academy/lesson/fundamental-attribution-error-definition-lesson-quiz.html)

Basing conclusions on mere observations of behavior is dangerous. As leaders, we sometimes become so frustrated by the ineffectiveness of others that we want something to explain the lack of success.

The problem isn't so much the lack of ministering activities; the problem is in the perception of the leader. Many leaders may perceive ministering as a very simple assignment. When ministering isn't done, those leaders cannot understand why someone can't simply pick up the phone, make a visit, send a text message, or greet their families at church. The leader, therefore, attributes it to laziness, bad attitudes, or lack of faith. We can't remedy lack of ministering until our perception of the problem is accurate.

Have you ever quietly thought the following to yourself?

> *"They don't minister because they don't know how to prioritize."*
> *"Every week members are late. They must not understand the importance of sacrament meeting."*
> *"We've knocked on their door for three months in a row. They must not want visitors."*
> *"Every time I ask him to do something, he drops the ball. He must not care."*

You can thank the *Fundamental Attribution Error* for this type of thinking.

How do we avoid the *Fundamental Attribution Error?*

According to the authors of *Crucial Conversations,* we need to ask ourselves a question. "Why would a reasonable, rational, and decent person act this way?" Keep this question in the back of your mind at all times. You will be shocked by how applicable it is to situations that raise your level of frustration. Some leaders may argue out of frustration that the sisters or brothers in their Relief Society or quorums are reasonable or rational, and I am sure most would say those members are decent people.

Consider this example: Larry is a lifelong member of The Church of Jesus Christ of Latter-day Saints who has served a mission and has three children. He has a college degree and is currently working on a master's degree in businesses administration. He is raising three children and often gets home late in the evening. When he sits down with his elders quorum president for his quarterly ministering interview and the elders quorum president asks him for his report, Larry has nothing to report. He didn't make any effort to contact his assigned ministering families, but he thinks maybe in the coming weeks he can make some time. Would it make sense for the leader to label him as lazy? Of course not. Larry is anything but lazy. Should he prioritize his time better? Possibly, but he is still having a positive impact on individuals in his family outside of his ministering assignment.

Elder David A. Bednar said the following about lazy home teachers

> *"Men in the Church who do not perform their priesthood duty as home teachers are not lazy; they simply have not understood the relevant doctrine and principles. Such men undoubtedly have been both taught and told. They may know that a home teacher is to watch over, be with, and strengthen (see Doctrine and Covenants 20:53)—but they have not learned, they do not understand, and they are not intelligent (as the word intelligence is used in the scriptures)"* (Increase in Learning, *p.124)*

Consider that quote the next time your human nature tells you people are lazy. Realize there is a doctrinal misunderstanding and teaching the doctrine can be the main focus of your quorum meetings. Once individuals gain a witness of that doctrine, the motivation will surface, and they will be willing to do uncomfortable things.

Is there REALLY a Motivation Problem?

Whenever I hear a group of people, mainly leaders, talk about how to improve ministering, more often than not someone will bring up the importance of *accountability*. "These members need to be held accountable each month, and that will get them visiting!" As I have discussed in earlier chapters, I am a huge proponent of accountability. Unfortunately, accountability is only one side of the solution. If the leader only holds people accountable, that is like trying to win a football game by only allowing your offense on the field.

When an individual appears not to be ministering, the leader begins to make certain judgments. He begins to wonder why the good sister or brother isn't doing what she or he isn't completing assignments. The default assumption (or fundamental attribution error) is to blame it on the individual's motivation. Here we have an elder in the Church, a man ordained with the authority of God and he can't seem to get himself off the couch to visit a poor widow. What can be done? How can we change this? We must infuse him with a deeper level of motivation! He must not understand the blessings, or rather; he must not understand the CONDEMNATION that will be on his soul for not ministering. The leader's knee-jerk reaction is to spiritually slap him until he awakens with the motivation to minister.

Is this an extreme example? Yes, but leaders attribute poor performance to a lack of *motivation*. In their effort to understand why someone is falling short leaders are only building one side of the boat and that boat will never float. Motivation is half of the problem—*ability* is the other half. They may be motivated, but they don't know *how* to minister.

One day, during the time of the home teaching program, I received an email from a discouraged home teacher who lives in a far-away state. He said, "I want to be a good home teacher. I work 60-plus hours each week and teach Sunday School. I assist in any service project I can, but I still can't get out and home teach. I live in a rural area. Our home teaching area covers hundreds of miles, some on dirt roads. I suffer from a debilitating illness, so I am tired all the time. I truly want to care for the families, but by the time I am home, it is impossible. What can I do?"

Does a man that works 60 hours a week sound like someone who is lazy or unmotivated? He loves his religion. He participates as a teacher on Sunday and probably needs a good amount of time for lesson preparation. His high level of motivation is without question, or else he would have never have sent such an email. The reality is, he didn't know HOW to home teach.

In the context of ministering, this might be a hard perspective for a leader to grasp. What do you mean he doesn't know how to minister? It's not quantum physics! It is even easier now to minister than it was to home teach! Everyone can accomplish such a task. Pick up the phone, send a text message, cook some brownies, and then go visit!

In Doctrine & Covenants 43:8 we are taught "that when [we] are assembled together [we] shall *instruct* and *edify* each other" (emphasis added). These two words, *instruct* and *edify* are respectively related to *ability* and *motivation*. Generally, in meetings that leaders run, they simply *edify* individuals with lessons that easily edify the group and invite the spirit. As leaders, we feel like we have done our job because we gave the elders an edifying quorum meeting that was motivational. But, as they leave the classroom, they may not know how to apply the teachings effectively because they were not *instructed* effectively—all motivation, and no ability.

For many people who have home taught for a long time, it is hard to understand this lack of ability. Imagine teaching someone with no experience how to play basketball by simply telling him, "All you need to do is take this round ball and put it in that basket." You then sub them in during an intense church ball game and wonder why they are not "putting the round ball into the basket." It is easy to see ministering as a very basic task that does not need instruction or practice. "All you need to do is take this list of names and start ministering!" Some need very little direction, but others would be no better off than the rookie basketball player.

I suggest that the majority of people who don't attempt ministering have an ability deficit and not a motivation deficit. Here are some examples of what that might look like:

- Being new in the ward Brother Jones doesn't know how to approach his ministering companion.
- Knocking on a door and leading a discussion with a ward member has always been difficult for Brother Altamirano. His throat gets dry, and he doesn't know what to say.
- Since Brother Christian works in the evening, he doesn't know how to fit ministering into his schedule.
- Brother Haynie always forgets to minister. If only he had a leader who would show him how to set a calendar reminder so that he remembers to make some calls each Sunday.

These are all very valid reasons someone may lack the

ability to act. Even in the most motivated state, the lack of ability can begin to drain motivational energy. Though lack of ability is a major factor in ministering, we should not dismiss a lack of motivation. There is a percentage of people in the group who do not find intrinsic satisfaction in interjecting themselves in the lives of others. In those situations, personal motivation is needed to create effective influence.

How to Change People Who Don't Want to Change

Lack of ability and understanding aren't always the reasons for lack of ministering; it can be motivation. So how do you motivate individuals to change when they have many reasons not to change? Maybe they sincerely don't feel a reason to minister. They have a testimony, they do those things that seem "vital" for their salvation, but if a few months go by and nobody on their list gets a visit, they don't feel like serious consequence will follow.

There have been some interesting studies done on human nature and how to motivate people who don't want to change. *VitalSmarts* (a training and development consulting firm) did an experiment related to smoking addicts. You probably don't have too many smoking addicts in your Relief Society or elders quorum, but this experiment is still quite telling when it comes to how to motivate people to minister. You can find the details about their study at crucialskills.com by searching "How to Change People Who Don't Want to Change."

VitalSmarts started this experiment on the premise that you can either "tell" someone to change, or you can "ask" someone to change. More often than not, society is *telling* smokers to quit. It is not hard to find anti-smoking billboards with black lungs displayed, or commercials showing the dire effects of emphysema. "If you don't stop smoking, you'll end up like me!" I have no doubt these advertisements are effective, but *VitalSmarts* wanted to see if *asking* would be better than *telling*. Most smokers don't need more information. They realize their lungs are going to turn black and they have a very high chance of lung cancer. It is about awakening the motivation already inside of them so they can put it into action.

To do this, *VitalSmarts* sent out two boys (probably about ten years old) to the streets of Salt Lake City, Utah to approach smokers with the intent to *tell* them to quit, and then they would try to *ask* them to quit.

Here's what happened…

The young boys approached a smoker (in the act of smoking) and lectured him on why he should stop. "Hey, you know smoking is bad for you?" They then offered the smokers a flier with information about how to quit. Guess how many of the smokers refused the information? Over 90% responded resentfully.

Later the boys tried replacing a "tired lecture" with an "influential question." They didn't just ask the smokers, "Would you please quit smoking?" Instead, they used a question that would stir up natural motivation in the smoker. The young boys approached the smoker with a fake cigarette and asked for a light. You can imagine these smokers being shocked that such a young boy was asking for help to smoke the cigarette. The amazing part of this experiment then happened when the smokers began to tell the boys why they shouldn't smoke. In the midst of these smokers' lectures, the young boys turned it back on the smokers. The boys asked, "If you care about us, what about you?" The body language of these smokers completely changed from the prior *telling* attempt. The smokers were much more positive and open to the boys. Ninety percent of the smokers they approached with the *asking* method committed to quitting smoking.

Other social scientists have conducted similar experiments and found that this motivation through *asking* lasts much longer than the interaction of *telling*. When this experiment was conducted in Bangkok, Thailand, calls to the *smoking quit line* went up by 40%.

Applying the Ask/Tell Approach to Ministering

Many Relief Society and elders quorum presidents think that to awaken motivation; a person needs more information. Needing motivation is not the same as needing information. So, don't offer more information about why the ministering program is inspired, or why an elderly lady down the street needs a visit. The ministering sisters or brothers already know the why. If you offer information that they already have, this may cause resistance, and they are more prone to push the leader away and dismiss those efforts. Don't lecture, as lecturing someone generally results in a defensive response. Ask questions and create a safe environment to explore the motivations they already have.

Suppose a Relief Society or elders quorum president is sitting down in a ministering interview to talk to an individual or companionship about the lack of ministering. He or she could easily lecture with statements like, "Don't you understand the Lord has asked us to minister to these families? Don't you understand the blessings that come from ministering?" That would be the typical lecture routine. Instead, the leader could ask thought-provoking questions that make it safe for the individual to provide feedback on the obstacles to ministering. "Did you ever home or visit teach as a youth? What are some things in your life that have changed since the time you did minister? If you could control your time and life exactly the way you wanted, do you think ministering would be a part of your schedule? Why? Why would you even want to minister? What makes it difficult to minister?

These types of questions bring their motivations to the surface. They create understanding, and the quorum member has great respect for his leader because he is *asking* rather than *telling*. The leader can offer himself as a resource to accomplish these inner motivations.

Influencing Change

When I was called as a young elders quorum president, I remember the discouraging feeling of sincerely having no clue what I was supposed to do. I wasn't trained in this field. I needed training—and I don't mean training on how to submit a report about my ministering interviews. I needed training in leading and influencing others! I wanted a recipe for how to influence others to be great ministering brothers. I needed a model that I could hold on to and reference when things weren't going well. There was nothing like this found in the handbooks of instruction, so I started reading and searching.

Then I found a model. There are many models to influencing change in a Relief Society or elders quorum, and I don't want to claim I have found the most superior. However, the *6-Source Model of Influence* is a solid model when it comes to leading a Relief Society and quorum. Credit for this model goes to *VitalSmarts*, a human behavior training, and development company in Orem, Utah, USA, which has done incredible research on the topic of influencing change. One can dive into this research by reading the book Influencer: *The New Science of Leading Change* (a must read for all leaders).

Having a model allows you to assess sub-par results. Like a game plan, if you walk off the field with a loss, the coaches can go back to the game plan and say, "We didn't execute here, here, and especially here."

Here is a visual representation of the 6-source model of influence:

	Motivation	Ability
Personal	1. Make the Undesirable Desirable	2. Surpass Your Limits
Social	3. Harness Peer Pressure	4. Find Strength in Numbers
Structural	5. Design Rewards and Demand Accountability	6. Change the Environment

Image: Vitalsmarts.com

You can see the dichotomy between motivation and ability in the model that I talked about before. We, as humans, do things that are difficult only when we are motivated to do them and only when we can do them. I may be motivated to lose weight, but if I don't know how to plan healthy meals and effectively exercise, it probably isn't going to happen. On the flip side, I may be able to minister, but I may not have the motivation to minister. As you can see at the top of the model, motivation, and ability are crucial components to understanding change.

To influence change in an organization, we need to understand that humans are motivated and enabled to do things on three different levels: *personal*, *social*, and *structural*.

Personal Level - "I have a testimony, so I *want* to minister to others, and I know how to build a relationship with someone so that I can minister."

Social Level - "I'm excited by the quorum vision, and I *want* to do my part to minister to others, so I want to get to know my ministering families. Plus, I am learning so much from my quorum president on *how* to minister that this should be easy."

Structural Level - "Brother Boutin lives right across the street from me, and I see him all the time. This should make it easy to begin getting to know him."

The benefit of having a model of influence to follow is that you can more easily find the reason someone is struggling with ministering. For example, let's say you sit down with a sister in your Relief Society who is discouraged (and a little ashamed) by the lack of ministering she has been doing over a four-month period. She doesn't feel close to her assigned sisters and isn't sure what to do next. You could then reference the 6-source model of influence and determine if the lack of motivation or ability is happening on a personal level, social level, or a structural level. After talking through each level with this sister, you realize she has such a hard time visiting her sisters because they live on the other side of the ward boundaries (15 miles away) and with her children's busy schedule she has a hard time finding time to visit those sisters who live so far away. This is a structural problem, and as the leader, you could discuss with her strategies that don't require her to visit them in their home like texting or calling, or you could consider assigning those sisters to someone in who lives closer.

Let's explore each of the 6-sources of influence in detail so that you can fully understand how to leverage this model to create positive change in the Relief Society or elders quorum.

Source 1 — Personal Motivation: Make the Undesirable Desirable

Making ministering intrinsically motivating would be ideal. We would all love to see ward members start to minister because they *want* to minister. When ministering becomes a chore, it may be rare to see sincere connection and friendship between the ministering sister/brother and their assigned families. As mentioned before, the majority of ministering sisters/brothers do not have a *personal motivation* problem related to ministering—it is more of an *ability* problem relating to their social and environmental surroundings. However, there is going to be a percentage of people in your group who do not find intrinsic satisfaction in finding ways to interject themselves in the life of others all to minister. In those situations, personal motivation is needed to create effective influence. Learning from the methods of *VitalSmarts*, in their book *Influencer* we gain suggestions on how to transform an undesirable action into something people are willing to do.

Get People to Try It

This strategy worked for me on my mission when I was encouraged to try the cow tongue taco. I tried it, and now I love cow tongue tacos. With ministering it is a matter of getting companionships out the door and visiting. This is typically done by pairing up the apathetic individual with someone more proactive and intentional. She or he will do all the scheduling, preparing, and then arrive at seven o'clock to pick up their companion. The strategy of pair-the-less-motivated-with-the-super-motivated has seemed to be the typical solution that has been tried for years. It may work in some cases but don't make it your only strategy. It also may require a counselor in the presidency to accompany the less-motivated individual on a few visits to help them get a feel for ministering or to determine what other reasons are discouraging this good person from ministering. Maybe one of the president's counselors is not assigned specific ministering families but instead is assigned to find the less motivated in the Relief Society or quorum and mentor them to minister more effectively and try it. Sounds like a great activity a counselor could do while the president focuses on ministering interviews. Through this process, the leader helps people get a taste of ministering and determine if they can find intrinsic motivation and ability to continue the task.

Connect Behaviors to Moral Values

Remember in chapter 1 when we discussed the importance of vision? The reason why a quorum vision is so important is that it connects moral values to the purpose of the quorum. Each individual in your quorum should also have a personal vision as it relates to ministering. Through the leader's ministering interviews, they may discover that an individual finds no purpose in ministering to families who seem to have life put together. The leader can help them find ways to minister as mentioned before or identify a few families whose specific needs allow a ministering sister/brother find value in their service

If an individual is struggling to connect their moral values to difficult tasks, he will be unlikely to exert the necessary effort towards the ministering task. Here are a few ways to connect ministering with an individual's moral values:

Consider assigning a family that truly needs help

As I just mentioned, if ministering to a family is difficult when there are few opportunities for service, assigning individuals to a family with specific needs may help the ministering sister/brother feel their service is needed. This could infuse them with motivation to minister and is another reason why it is important to prioritize the families in the ward depending on their immediate needs as discussed in chapter 2.

Humanize the problem

One Sunday during my time as a high priest group leader I invited a handful of sisters (mostly single sisters who benefited from home teaching) into our group meeting and simply had them share with the group the difference home teaching was making in their life. I remember each sister was brought to tears as they tried to adequately articulate the blessings they had received from faithful home teachers.

The purpose of this activity was to humanize the task and show them the difference their efforts made on a personal level. It's easy to see names on a list and forget that these are real people with real problems. It would be good practice to find ways for people to share ministering experiences in the Relief Society or quorum setting.

Source 2 — Personal Ability: Surpass Your Limits

In Source 1 we talked about how to influence someone's motivation, which is a big step. However, in most cases, it isn't motivation that is lacking. Remember the *fundamental attribution error?* We see that members of our Relief Society or quorum are not ministering, so we conclude it is because that they do not *want* to do it or they are lazy. We might also assume they never developed the social skills to minister effectively. What if in reality, they do not know *how* to minister? The attribution error happens when the experienced leader, who finds ministering quite simple, assumes the rest of the group has the same perspective.

Let's talk about a few tactics that can be used in the Influencer Source 2 concept.

Deliberate Practice

Consider our rookie basketball player again. You would not simply tell him to throw the ball at the basket until he learns the fundamentals of shooting. You would show him where to place his hands on the basketball, how to keep his arm straight, and his elbow tucked in. This is *deliberate practice*. The fundamentals are important in basketball and in ministering. The fundamentals in basketball may include: keep the shooting arm perpendicular, aim for the back of the rim; use the backboard for layups. The fundamentals in ministering may include: being intentional in seeking them out during church and having a short conversation, or praying for them each night by name, or setting reminders of their birthdays and other important family events, etc. During a ministering interview, it might make sense to spend the whole time discussing fundamentals required to minister effectively. You may discover a simple shortcoming in their fundamentals, and now you have a specific concept to coach.

Let's imagine you, as the Relief Society or elders quorum president are conducting a ministering interview to a less-effective ministering member. As you inquire about their lack of effort, they give you a typical excuse, "I just didn't get around to it." or "Life's been busy." This is the time to fight off the fundamental attribution error and start asking probing questions until you discover the fundamental ability that is lacking. Until you do this, you will have nothing to resolve—no place to offer to coach.

Provide Immediate Feedback

Once the member knows how to practice the fundamentals, he or she then needs feedback. This again shows the dramatic need for regular ministering interviews (with the same "coach"). By giving them constant feedback, it keeps them accountable and persistent. "So, tell me what happened when you made an effort to greet the Johnson family each Sunday? Did it work? What do you think you need to do next?" Even professional basketball players are receiving immediate feedback on their fundamentals—so should ministering brothers and sisters.

Break Mastery into Mini-Goals

Relief Society and quorum presidents are only required to do a ministering interview with one member of the companionship once a quarter. What do you think would happen if you approached that differently? Instead of waiting for your quarterly interview, what if you made ten lightning calls each week to ten different members of your group? In a few minutes, you could quickly make some mini-goals that they could accomplish that day or week to make a connection with their families?

Remember, focusing on personal ability is just one of six sources of influence to consider. You are not going to influence the level of ministering by focusing on personal ability alone. Once we review each of the six sources of influence, it will be clear how personal ability fits into finding the solution. Once personal motivation and ability are in place, we can then move on to factoring in social influences.

Sources 3 & 4 — Harness Peer Pressure & Find Strength in Numbers

Creating a group effort in programs like ministering is important because there is an obvious strength in numbers. There is a powerful African proverb that says, "If you want to go quickly, go alone. If you want to go far, go together." This is a great example of why it is so important to create a vision statement and focus together as a Relief Society or quorum. When everyone buys into a moment, it fuels itself and goes further than expected. There is strength in numbers when we harness peer influence.

The Power of Everyone

It's not about getting everyone to minister; it's about creating a movement (social motivation). This requires you to teach the Relief Society or quorum how to work as a team (social ability). When individuals are part of a movement, they do remarkable things to achieve the goal. This is the desire of all quorum presidents.

Once you have established a Relief Society or quorum vision statement during, a future lesson could focus on the ministering effort. Now that ministering has become more established, and it isn't just the "new program" that many are trying to figure out there is probably a lot of feedback members of your Relief Society or quorum are willing to share with you as the leader. Getting feedback could be stimulated by questions, including the following:

- Does the presidency assign ministering assignments effectively?
- Why does ministering feel empty at times?
- What would change if we stopped ministering?
- What do *you* want out of home teaching?

Get to the heart of the matter and create safety in the discussion by not dismissing perspectives. Let them know it is okay to criticize the methods of the presidency in this setting so that we can discover new ideas and to further understand their perspective. When safety is established, they might say phrases like, "I hate the nagging from the quorum presidency." "It is frustrating when my ministering assignments change every other month." "I don't think anything is being accomplished through ministering. I ask my assigned families what we can do for them, and they say they don't need anything."

When you start having an honest discussion with your quorum, you begin fixing the problem as a group and move towards a solution together. When you have a solution that was discovered as a group, motivation will follow. You now have an army that is fighting for the same cause.

Source 5 — Design Rewards & Demand Accountability

"How about a pizza party? An ice cream party? A big yellow star on your forehead?"

Many Latter-day Saint leaders have experimented with incentives and rewards — and many do so at their peril. I heard of many examples of rewarding a group of people back when home and visiting teaching was the focus and it never seemed to motivate in the right way. That doesn't mean rewards or incentives should be thrown out when a leader is attempting to motivate a group.

Reward Vital Behaviors, Not Just Results

Incentives are not totally off the table when it comes to ministering, but it isn't what you think. I'm not suggesting you stand in front of your quorum with homemade cookies and pass them out to anyone who has done a ministering activity that week. What I am saying is that you highlight specific vital behaviors that individuals are taking that lead to effective ministering relationships. What is a vital behavior? A vital behavior is an action that someone has complete control over that has shown to lead to the desired outcome. For example, there are many variables in achieving a happy marriage. The husband or the wife doesn't have control over every event that happens in their life that might cause stress or argument in the relationship; however, if the husband washing the dishes daily, and scrubs the toilets weekly then their marriage is most likely going to improve (believe me, I speak from experience). These are vital behaviors.

In an elders quorum setting, you might identify specific behaviors like sending a weekly text, making a regular visit to their home, taking them brownies, etc. (you can look at the 101 ways to minister list in chapter 4 for more ideas). Again, you aren't looking to give them extrinsic rewards like cookies or a big star on their forehead. Instead, focus on intrinsic rewards. This often comes in the form of recognition. During quorum meeting recognize specific individuals by having them share a positive experience they had ministering to another (it doesn't have to be with their assigned families). When recognizing an individual in front of their peers, it becomes more rewarding than any slice of pizza.

Take time to thank the individual personally outside of your formal ministering interview. It might be when you pass them in the hall or by sending a simple text message. Be specific about what you noticed about their ministering efforts.

Celebrate every bit of progress. As you meet on Sunday, when appropriate, highlight the change that has taken place in the lives of specific families in the ward because of ministering efforts. It might be helping with a move, or seeing someone interact with others in the foyer. It doesn't have to be momentous. By recognizing the simple moments of ministering you feed the culture of ministering that everyone wants to be a part of.

Source 6 — Change the Environment

As the adage says, "fish are the last to discover water." The same is true for how we interact with our environment. We often underestimate the influence that our environment has on us. If you are ever frustrated in the progress of your Relief Society or quorum ministering it would be worth your time to consider how the environment or context of the assignment if impacting those you lead. It's not all about personal and social motivation.

Here are a few approaches to consider to leverage the environment or structure of your ministering to make it easier on those striving to minister.

Make the Invisible Visible

Consider the ward list that most members of the Church use in the Member Tools smartphone app. What percentage of the membership of the ward has a recent photo of themselves and their family attached to their records? When someone receives a new assignment to minister, it would be very beneficial if they can go to the app and have a visual of who they are. It's simple but extremely helpful to activate someone into ministering.

Surrounding Space

It is time to come back to the word *propinquity*—which is another way to refer to physical proximity. The same power that makes you work out more often because your treadmill is in front of the TV also works for ministering. Where things are located and how they relate plays a large role in whether someone is visited or receives ministering. I mentioned this earlier in the book but, the fact that someone has to drive 45 minutes to interact with someone they are assigned to might be a huge barrier. Sure, they can call or text them, but the more individuals can naturally interact with those they minister to day-to-day the more likely the ministering effort will work. Consider where people live or personal interests when making ministering assignments.

Considering proximity becomes vital when a disaster hits and people need to know who is closest to them and in the most need.

Make it easy

Many times, the solution to motivating and enabling others to be effective ministers is in sight so plainly that you can't see it at all. This is why I mentioned in chapter 2 some easy ways to leverage established friendships in ministering. If they are already good friends, make them good ministering brothers or sisters. When they get sick, they tell their friend. They visit them many times a month.

They already have a relationship of trust and always receive a call in times of need. Some friends don't cover all these bases, but when they receive the assignment to be their ministering sister brother, it won't take much additional effort. The more friends they have on their list, the less likely they will feel like they are on assignment.

When seeking vital change never forget about a quorum members' environment.

Establishing a Ministering Strategy

As I mentioned before, the 6-Source model of influence is a simple model that can help leaders and ministering brothers and sisters put together an influence strategy to help them accomplish their goal. It's based around the *why* (motivation) and the *how* (ability). Those are both helpful targets to focus on, but many times you will find that members of your Relief Society or quorum are motivated and able, but they don't know *what* to do minister. This will require you as a leader to help the group or specific individuals to put together a strategy to feed their motivation and ability. Let's talk about a few strategic approaches to ministering.

Leveraging Opening Exercises

I remember walking into priesthood opening exercises as a newly ordained deacon back in 1994. I am not sure of the overall purpose of this meeting, but it is ingrained in our Latter-day Saint meeting habits. From what I understand the women have a similar routine in Relief Society. Many times, priesthood opening exercises seem like a quick touchpoint of a hymn, prayer, and announcements. Then there are a few snarky comments from random participants that make the room rumble in old man laughter. Finally, there's the round-robin where we check in with the deacons quorum president, teachers quorum president, elders quorum president, and anyone else with some level of authority to give an announcement to the body.

As an elders quorum president, I have seen this short kick-off meeting as a time when I have the majority of elders in the room, including those who serve in the Young Men's program. I rarely have a specific "announcement" as elders quorum president, so I take the opportunity to pull out my 101 ministering ideas list from chapter 4 and give the quorum members an idea of how they can minister that day or the following week. This draws everyone's attention to their list of names and hopefully gives them a chance to be prompted by the Spirit. I've done everything from encouraging them to send a text to their ministering families, to having everyone pull out their smartphone so I could show them how to find their ministering assignments in the Member Tools app. So, take a minute each week to give people the *what* of their ministering strategy.

Non-Members

The Power of Everyday Missionaries, by Clayton Christensen, is by far one of my favorite books on missionary work. There is a great story in that book that applies so much to ministering. I'll share the except here:

> *I was the home teacher to an elderly woman in our ward. On a Saturday in July we experienced the worst of Boston's weather: The temperature was nearly 100 degrees F., and the humidity was above 90 percent. It was miserable. I decided that I had better visit Julia to be sure that she was okay. When I went into her home, I exclaimed to Julia, who had lost her sense of smell, "Something has died in this house! It smells awful." We followed the smell into her basement, where we saw the problem. The prior Christmas, her son who lived in Florida had shipped a case of grapefruit to his mother. Julia had put the case into an old refrigerator in her basement and then had forgotten that it was there. A bit later she heard an advertisement suggesting that*

unused appliances should be turned off. So, Julia went right down and unplugged the refrigerator. Over the subsequent months the fruit had rotted, and the mold was everywhere. "Julia, we need to get this out of your house and get it to the dump," I told her.

I went home and phoned through the ward list, but nobody was available. Desperate, I asked a nonmember neighbor, Jim, to help. Several times previous to this I had asked Jim whether he might be interested to learn a bit about our wonderful church, but Jim had always kindly deflected my invitations. But to this call for help, he readily responded.

Not only was it hot and humid that day, but the task took two hours of hard work. The old fridge was heavy—made of cast iron, as best we could tell. It was wider than Julia's rickety basement staircase, which had two right-angle turns in it. So, we had to take off the railings, and with WD-40 we got the door off the fridge. Soon our clothes were soaked with perspiration. When we reached the first turn in the staircase and had balanced the fridge on the landing, Jim said, "So, tell me about the Mormon church."

Mopping my brow, I responded, "Frankly, Jim, like it or not, this is the Mormon church." I then explained how home teaching worked, noted how much this sister needed us, and illustrated how our own home teacher helped our family. I also told him that because graduate students and their families were moving in and out of our area all the time, our family was often helping someone load or unload a rental truck.

Jim was incredulous. "At our church we just listen to the sermon and go home. I have no idea who might need my help, and there is no way that they might know whether I needed their help. I like this kind of thing. The next time one of you Mormons needs help, will you ask me?

Although I had tried to engage Jim in discussions about religion in the past, Jim was uninterested. But he was interested in opportunities to help others. Jim felt something that he had rarely felt in his church, and he subsequently accepted our invitation to take the missionary discussions.

I love reflecting on that story because it helps me realize how lucky we are as Latter-day Saints to have an inspired program that gets us moving and gets us serving others who we would never know had a need.

As leaders, it is important that we engage those in our Relief Society or quorum and determine how we can involve non-members in this effort. The ward mission leader will love you for this focus. Not only should individuals consider the non-members around their home and try to be aware of their needs, but they should also consider calling them when there is a need in the ward. It's easy to go down the ward list to find helpers for a move, but consider making a personal list of non-members around your home by asking them directly if they would be willing to serve others in the area when a need arises.

Another great resource around the topic is *The Art of Neighboring*, by Dave Runyon and Jay Pathak. You can listen to a motivating interview with Dave Runyon on the Leading Saints podcast at LeadingSaints.org.

A Word on Unity

The purpose of this chapter is to discuss strategies that will produce results through motivating and enabling those you lead. No doubt, unity of your Relief Society or quorum will play an important role. It is easy for a Relief Society or quorum meeting to become very routine and empty since the only time we interact with one another is during the third hour of church each week. I had this realization a few weeks into my most recent call as elders quorum president. I was striving to create a grand movement of ministering as a quorum, and all we do is sit in a room together once a week. That model will not create the unity necessary to establish a strong vision and create influence.

So, what is a leader to do? Well, it reminds me of a young single adult ward in Utah that had the highest marriage rate out of any other YSA ward in the surrounding area. The bishop of the ward credited the high marriage rate to "service activities." He didn't worry about the cute Family Home Evening activities where speed dating took place, or where groups decorated sugar cookies together with the hope that men and women would socialize, date, and then marry. This bishop simply focused on creating activities of service. Being engaged in service simulated individuals being engaged in marriage. When we serve together as a Relief Society or quorum, we become more unified. So, don't assume more activities or more basketball nights will do the trick; it takes more consistent activities of service to bring a quorum together and establish the unity necessary to create influence and accomplish your vision.

This doesn't mean you have to have huge service activities. It could be simple micro-activities that take little planning but get people in a room together doing simple acts of service like writing missionaries, fixing a neighbor's rain gutter, or setting up chairs for the next priesthood meeting. Many of these activities don't require the entire Relief Society or quorum to be present but even if a handful of people are present and serving it will lead to positive, unifying results.

CONCLUSION/AFTERWORD

"Culture eats strategy for breakfast." It's unclear who said this first, but most people attribute this quote to Peter Drucker, a management thinker. Regardless who said it, this is one of the main points to take away from this book. Your objective as a leader is not to manipulate people into ministering to others; instead, you are creating a culture of ministering. Creating a culture is the hardest thing you will ever do as a leader, but it is crucial for any organization. You don't want people to act because they were asked to act, you want people to act because something inside of them has changed and they can't help but act. That is the message of the gospel.

Establishing a strong positive culture in a Relief Society and quorum lasts long after the leader is released. It creates a feeling that every succeeding leader wants to adopt and continue. Culture isn't something that needs to be explained to the "new guy or gal" on his first week in quorum meeting or at the first Relief Society activity. Culture is something he or she will feel right away. Not only will they feel it, but they will desire to be a part of it.

I remember a time when I served as bishop. We had a

particularly heavy welfare month. A lot of financial requests were coming in, and they all seemed very sincere. This wasn't a complete surprise considering I was serving in an inner-city ward in South Salt Lake with a consistent welfare load. It became my heaviest responsibility as a bishop. On this particular week, I stood in the clerk's office holding a stack of envelopes that were addressed to landlords, apartment buildings, and utility companies. These were checks I had signed that were headed to buy families and individuals one more month of survival. The decisions leading up to signing these checks were difficult. Whenever I would make a final welfare decision, I would often think of those members approaching me on Sunday with a gray donation envelope. Every one of those envelopes probably held tithing money, but a number of them held fast offering funds as well, and it was up to me, the only person holding the keys to make such a decision, to determine how those funds were used. I felt accountable to those contributing members. Many of those members giving should have been the ones receiving. So, when it came time to sign those checks and officially use that money, I felt like I needed to decide with the highest level of certitude, and do so before the rent was late. Standing there with that stack of envelopes I said, under my breath, "I hate this job." In an instant, I felt the Spirit rebuke me. How could I hate a job where I was helping so many people? How could I utter such a phrase when I was entrusted with such responsibility?

This welfare responsibility became even more difficult when I had to tell people, "NO." Many times, because of poor decisions people made, I couldn't justify using the sacred fast offering funds to support them another month. I had to tell many people they would need to move in with friends or family, or call the homeless shelter until they found a permanent living situation. Seeing these individuals leave my bishop's office, many times they were angry with me, I felt like I had ruined them. I hadn't been able to fix their situation or offer them better help.

This feeling of failure is what many Relief Society and elders quorum presidents feel when they have worked so hard to establish ministering in their groups but have failed to see any change or improvement. I hope the lessons in this book have given you some ideas to try. I hope you have a renewed effort to keep striving to find success. But I also know that you might face disappointment again and be tempted to lose hope and label everyone "lazy."

If I could emphasize any lesson to take from this book, it is, **you were not called to fix it.** This isn't your church. This is the Church of Jesus Christ. This is God's Kingdom on Earth, and he called you to be a leader. The Lord has the power to save those individuals not being visited. Christ's Atonement doesn't only visit once a month. It visits every second of every minute. Give the burden to Him and then get back to work establishing a culture of ministering.

EPILOGUE: MY TESTIMONY

As I have shared this manuscript with others, I am encouraged when I hear people disagree with a tactic or approach that I have shared. My intention in writing this book is not to claim I have found the one true way of effectively leading the ministering effort; rather, it is to share my experience as someone who has tried to lead and to share the experience of others who I have interviewed or who have published their perspective on leading others. Even if you read this book and disagree with every point in these pages, I still count it as a success because hopefully, it has caused you to step back and analyze your leadership approaches and maybe try a new, more effective approach.

I love leadership. I love the context in which someone can develop as a leader in The Church of Jesus Christ of Latter-day Saints. As I have heard it said, the lay leadership of the Church is one of the most miraculous modern-day miracles that we can daily witness as we see the "weak and simple" placed in positions of influence. They grow and develop into sanctified individuals in a way that could only happen through the opportunity to lead.

At the end of most interviews on the Leading Saints podcast, I ask the question, "How has being a leader made you a better follower of Jesus Christ." To me, that is the essence of all leadership in the church. It isn't so much that we become great leaders so that we can have all the answers or fix all the problems; rather, it's about serving in a way that results in us following the Savior more intentionally.

This has been my experience. In the quiet moments of the toughest leadership decisions I have ever had to make, I have felt a sustaining that can only come from an immortal source. Though I have never seen an angel or had the heavens open before me, I feel the tremble of a distant crowd of angels encouraging me on as I strive to lead the best I can. This gospel has taught me in incredible ways to trust in God, to press on, to remain optimistic, and most importantly, to love those around me. I turn to the Book of Mormon and other scriptures for inspiration and comfort as I read the stories of other inexperienced leaders striving to do their best in carrying out the work of the Lord.

Thank you for reading this book and considering my ideas and perspectives. Now the task is in your hands. I hope you feel an extra level of strength to stand in confidence as you lead, knowing you have been set-apart with power beyond this world to lead effectively.

As always, remember to *be a leader and not a calling.*

ABOUT THE AUTHOR

Kurt Francom is the founder and executive director of Leading Saints, a nonprofit organization helping lay leaders be prepared to lead. He manages the day-to-day efforts of Leading Saints and is the host of the podcast by the same name. Kurt currently lives in Woods Cross, Utah with his lovely wife Alanna. They are blessed to have two children (girl and boy). He enjoys drawing caricatures, basketball, reading, and college football. Kurt has served as a full-time missionary (California Sacramento), an elders quorum president (2005), bishopric counselor, bishop, and stake presidency first counselor. He currently serves as an elders quorum president.

ABOUT LEADING SAINTS

Leading Saints is a nonprofit organization with a mission to enhance leadership ability and capacity of lay religious leaders in order to accelerate the mission of The Church of Jesus Christ of Latter-day Saints. It was started in 2010 as a simple blog and has since developed into a popular podcast (2014) and then became a 501c3 non-profit (2016). Leading Saints reaches an international audience with over 1 million podcast downloads and 40,000 unique visitors to the website a month. You can find Latter-day Saint leadership content and learn more about the Leading Saints mission by visiting LeadingSaints.org.

Leading Saints is not owned or operated by The Church of Jesus Christ of Latter-day Saints.

Made in the USA
Las Vegas, NV
22 November 2021

35043836R00085